Palgrave Studies in Communication for Social Change

Series Editors
Pradip Ninan Thomas
The University of Queensland
Queensland, Australia

Elske van de Fliert
The University of Queensland
Queensland, Australia

Communication for Social Change (CSC) is a defined field of academic enquiry that is explicitly transdisciplinary and that has been shaped by a variety of theoretical inputs from a variety of traditions, from sociology and development to social movement studies. The leveraging of communication, information and the media in social change is the basis for a global industry that is supported by governments, development aid agencies, foundations, and international and local NGOs. It is also the basis for multiple interventions at grassroots levels, with participatory communication processes and community media making a difference through raising awareness, mobilising communities, strengthening empowerment and contributing to local change. This series on Communication for Social Change intentionally provides the space for critical writings in CSC theory, practice, policy, strategy and methods. It fills a gap in the field by exploring new thinking, institutional critiques and innovative methods. It offers the opportunity for scholars and practitioners to engage with CSC as both an industry and as a local practice, shaped by political economy as much as by local cultural needs. The series explicitly intends to highlight, critique and explore the gaps between ideological promise, institutional performance and realities of practice.

More information about this series at
http://www.springer.com/series/14642

Aristea Fotopoulou

Feminist Activism and Digital Networks

Between Empowerment and Vulnerability

Aristea Fotopoulou
University of Brighton
Brighton, United Kingdom

Palgrave Studies in Communication for Social Change
ISBN 978-1-137-50470-8   ISBN 978-1-137-50471-5 (eBook)
DOI 10.1057/978-1-137-50471-5

Library of Congress Control Number: 2016958806

Cover illustration: © 1Apix / Alamy Stock Photo

Printed on acid-free paper

This Palgrave Macmillan imprint is published by Springer Nature
The registered company is Macmillan Publishers Ltd.
The registered company address is: The Campus, 4 Crinan Street, London, N1 9XW, United Kingdom

PROLOGUE

This book is about digital networks, feminist networks and the spaces in between. It is about nodes and bonds, ties and knots, threads and loops, the things that connect us and those that break us. It is a book about politics and its attachments, about the materiality of affect and everyday practices and about the importance of social life and friendship. It is about gendered bodies that sweat, move and sigh, bodies that type, click and labour in front of a screen, bodies that get angry, get disappointed and have hopes. Above all, this book is about contradiction and tension, empowerment and vulnerability.

It is also a book about continuity and change. It started as a Ph.D. research project and transformed into a book, with a few years' pause. Many things changed in digital media during this pause; I bought a smartphone and used a fitness wearable device; social media sparked revolutions; airbnb became a verb. And suddenly, we were postdigital. I am aware that linear time is not friends with research about technological change. But like bodies, ideas too need to breathe and stretch. They stretch deeper in the past, to what it felt like to be the 8-year-old girl who coded with BASIC in 1983, to get connected to BBSs in 1987; to partition your hard drive in 1993 and set up webpages just for fun in 1996. For this feminist geek, by 1999, the internet had lost its novelty, but the social transformations of the digital were just starting to unravel.

From subjective experience to performative moment, this book is an enactment of connections and relations. I am indebted to the activists and research participants who shared their stories and time with me, most of whom will remain anonymous: Beatrix Campbell, Carry Hamilton, Anna van Heeswijk, Katrin Jacobs, Finn Mackay, Rebecca Morden, Susie Orbach and Lizzie Thynne. I am also thankful to the Brighton Ourstory project for access to their important archive of local lesbian, gay, bisexual and transgender (LGBT) history.

I am deeply grateful to many colleagues and friends for discussing some of the ideas that appear in this book. Special thanks to Caroline Bassett and Kate O'Riordan, my thesis supervisors, and my viva voce examiners Sally Munt and Sarah Kember. Many of the arguments in this book are around sustaining feminist knowledge in digital media, which I explored further in the research project Susnet (Sustaining Networked Knowledge: Expertise, Feminist Media Production), which was supported by the EPSRC Digital Economy Communities and Culture Network. Susnet culminated to the conference Queer Feminist and Social Media Praxis, which I organised with the support of the Sussex Centre for Cultural Studies at the University of Sussex, and with the help of Cynthia Weber, Laura Sjoberg and Heidi Hudson, from the *International Feminist Journal of Politics*. I am indebted to my co-editors Alex Juhasz and Kate O'Riordan of the special issue *of ADA: Journal of Gender, New Media and Technology*, entitled Queer, Feminist Media Praxis, to all the contributing authors and to the FemBot Collective for many inspiring exchanges. I would like to acknowledge the influence of my colleagues at the Sociology Department in Lancaster University, despite the shortness of my stay there, especially Debra Ferreday, Anne Marie Fortier, Maureen McNeill and Imogen Tyler. My thinking has also been shaped by the fascinating discussions I had with scholars in the Centre for Cultural Studies, History of Consciousness, and Science and Justice, during my visiting fellowship at the University of California, Santa Cruz. I am indebted to many colleagues in the field for their intellectual engagement, particularly in the conferences of Feminist and Women's Studies Association (FWSA), and the European Communication Research and Education Association (ECREA). I would especially like to acknowledge Nick Couldry's deep influence on my writing and thinking about the social. During my postdoc at Goldsmiths College, University of London, and after, he has acted as an important mentor. My new intellectual home, the University of Brighton, has provided me with an environment of collegiality, essential for completing the manuscript of the book. I am particularly grateful to Ryan Burns and Paula Hearsum for their flexibility and support. I would also like to thank Irene Fubara-Manuel and Lefteris

Zenerian for their help with the bibliography. Special thanks to Rosalind Gill, Carol Stabile and again Nick Couldry, for reading the manuscript and providing such kind endorsements.

Some of the material in this book has appeared in other forms: a version of Chapter 2 was originally published in New Media & Society in 2014; some material from Chapter 3 has been published in the Journal of Lesbian Studies, 17 (3–4), 253–266; and a very early and quite different version of Chapter 5 has been published in the ECREA book Communicative approaches to politics and ethics in Europe, edited by Nico Carpentier et al. (2009).

Finally, my greatest thanks goes to my family. Georgia and Demos Fotopoulos have always encouraged me to walk my own path. My brother Charis, who told me bedtime stories about Silicon Valley and taught me how to fight back, will never read this book, but it would make him glad, I am sure. I honour him in every single page of this book. I am infinitely thankful to Hilde C. Stephansen, who has tirelessly read and edited. Her grammar purism and critical intellectual comments have greatly benefited this book. She has supported me generously in so many precious ways during the time it took me to complete this book and has always been there. I am grateful to have you in my life. And my son Erik Demos has been patient with me while I worked weekends for this book, and has made this world joyful. Thank you.

CONTENTS

LIST OF FIGURES

CHAPTER 1

Introduction: Conceptualising Feminist Activism and Digital Networks

Feminist and queer activism are guided by strong visions of social change in which digital and network communications feature prominently. The invisibility, normalisation and ubiquity of media in our everyday lives, and the strong influence of imaginaries, make it important to question their role and impact on contemporary political identities and action. What does it mean for network technologies and network logics to become incorporated in the everyday lives and spaces of activists, as a preferred and often even default mode of interaction? Are these technologies just tools used concurrently with media and cultural forms of political expression that were dominant prior to Web 2.0,[1] e.g. protest marches, mailing lists and zines? Or do they reconfigure feminist politics and cultures in more fundamental ways?

In this book, I approach these questions by delineating digital networked culture as a space of tensions and contradictions. There are contradictions between inclusion and exclusion in new communicative environments; between representation and materiality; between articulations of opportunity and realisations of impossibility; and, perhaps the most important tension for activists in the digital era, between vulnerability and empowerment. These tensions and contradictions are prescribed by the ways in which our lives increasingly take place in digitally saturated environments – and by this I refer to both online spaces and the widespread digital saturation of virtually all aspects of our lives. But far from

© The Author(s) 2016
A. Fotopoulou, *Feminist Activism and Digital Networks*,
Palgrave Studies in Communication for Social Change,
DOI 10.1057/978-1-137-50471-5_1

assuming that digital technologies are the most central aspect of our cultural and political lives, and resisting the myth of the internet as a priori democratic, I maintain a focus on the embodied, lived, material and socially situated aspects of feminist and queer activism. Such attention involves a reflection on the intersections of age, class, race and disability in specific social and cultural contexts, and as they operate at larger scales online. Media technologies, social media and the internet do not exist as a space beyond and independently of the situated practices of feminist activists. They inform and shape each other. In fact, as I argue in this book, *doing feminism* and *being feminist* implies enacting ourselves primarily as embodied and social subjects through media practices and imaginaries of technologies and the internet, but also as citizens and users of these technologies.

In examining what forms of feminist and queer political engagement are culturally and historically specific in the context of networked communication, I find it necessary to think about political subjectivities and agency, and the media practices that inform them. What does it mean to be a feminist in the digital age and how do we understand being political? Posing this question entails resisting the assumption that feminism is one movement, or one unified identity. When talking about gender and sexuality politics, we need to be reminded of the immense diversity of feminist cultures, and the passionate commitment to self-reflexivity that characterises feminism as a social movement with a long history. These are key aspects of feminism that are especially neglected in accounts clinging to a taxonomy of waves. Feminist activism is not one thing. As I show in this book, it is a complex set of identities and cultures, whose different investments in, and practices with, media technologies mean different organisational structures and even political priorities. For some, social media and other new media technologies are strategic – they provide opportunities for direct engagement with civic life. For others, digital media delineate a space where certain gendered bodies, such as those of older women or trans people, experience new forms of precariousness and marginalisation. For example, in Chapter 2, I examine how women's groups, like other contemporary civil society actors, participate in the online public sphere (Downing 2001; Gordon 2007) to different degrees; age, lack of resources and media literacy are the three most important factors that modulate this participation, and in some cases become new types of exclusions of access to publicity and recognition. Being neither hackers nor artists, these activists could not really work 'through protocol'

(Galloway 2004) to achieve recognition. They lacked the necessary skills and resources that would allow them to resist the ubiquity of protocol. But the picture is very different for the so-called digital natives in many women's organisations that have emerged after the domestication of internet technologies and social media, and for whom media technologies are a form of cultural and social capital. Meanwhile, postporn transnational networks, geeky feminist cultures that use selfies as a political tool, queer feminists who create a pedagogic activist media practice and academic feminist networks whose focus is the production of knowledge are all different political formations entering the discussion of this book with different stakes and expectations from the digital. And we must not forget that this diversity of feminist cultures and identities operates within a wider cultural and political context of neoliberalism, in which discourses of autonomy and choice challenge any kind of collective identity.

Theoretically, the book sits within recent debates in critical social theory and network politics, which have well identified a decline in representation and traditional political life. Approached as part of technoscientific capitalism, digital network culture is often seen to contribute to this decline, because it is becoming increasingly difficult to form collective and sustained forms of politics in a culture that is characterised by ephemeral – though abundant – content production and circulation of media texts. However, it is not enough to denote such decline. I find it essential to identify and account for forms of organisation that have within them the potential for a progressive politics of social equality. In my project of mapping such politics, and the entanglement of feminism with communicative practices and paradigms, I rework notions of biopolitics in digital networks, mainly through the work of Hardt and Negri, and Terranova; while I am informed by key concepts in feminist science and technology studies from key theorists, including Barad, Braidotti, Colebrook and Haraway. In thinking about feminist politics and digital media, I start my exploration in this book with emphasis on

- situated activist media practices,
- the relationship between activism and communicative capitalism and
- the cultural/historical contexts and social visions shaping this feminism and their digital media practices.

My aim is twofold: first, since this is an empirically informed project, I seek to provide a substantial but by no means exhaustive account of contemporary gender and sexual politics, and to understand how ideas of networks, citizenship and community are perceived by activists. Second, the book theorises the interchange between digital media and feminism and develops a set of interdisciplinary analytical tools for future research, by drawing critically from existing innovative research in the fields of media theory, political science and feminist science and technology studies. The first one, *networked feminism*, describes the collective identities and communicative practices of activists as they are shaped by the social imaginary of the internet (understood as *the* network) and digital engagement. The concept of networked feminism helps us rethink media technologies and their role in feminism by reflecting on how activist cultures negotiate five key aspects of digital media technologies: access, connectivity, immediacy, labour and visibility. Through these negotiations, activists critically rethink and problematise rather than accept digital media as intrinsically exploitative or empowering technologies. *Biodigital vulnerability* helps us understand the complex dynamics of content production and control that constitute online networks as contradictory spaces of both vulnerability and empowerment for feminist and queer politics. In particular, my argument is that corporeal vulnerability, and the new forms of governmentality that appear due to technoscientific acceleration, when made public can have great political potential and can be empowering for communities and individuals that have been marginalised or victimised due to sexuality or gender. But let me start by clarifying some of the key theoretical premises of the book.

Digital Feminism?

Following the more generalised optimism about the role of social media in uprisings around the world such as those in Tunisia and Egypt, many writers have celebrated digital feminist activism as a turning point for feminism as a social movement, particularly because of its seeming horizontality and capacity to facilitate intersectional debate.[2] An article in *The Guardian* has gone as far as to exclaim that digital media technologies are so important to building a strong and reactive movement that they signify a 'fourth wave' in the feminist movement (Cochrane 2013). The hopefulness regarding social media and their capacity to facilitate feminist activism is by no means unsubstantiated. There are, indeed, many examples of feminist activism happening online since 2010 to draw from: Twitter actions and hashtag feminism in relation to the actions of PussyRiot are perhaps the most popular and recognisable ones. But even less prominent cases, such as FEMEN, have been considered to operate as reflexive critical spaces where tensions such as those arising from white privilege can be revisited. In an examination of Slutwalk Berlin, FEMEN, and Muslima Prida, and the associated hashtags, Baer (2015), for instance, notes how these digital feminist campaigns make visible the tensions that have characterised feminism as a social movement for years. But Baer (2015) goes as far as calling this a 'redoing of feminism', because of the interplay between local embodied struggles, protest and the more discursive and disembodied activity online. One may here recognise a response to Angela Mcrobbie's (2007) key argument that neoliberalism and post-feminism in particular are 'undoing feminism'. This optimistic response to a bleak diagnosis is attractive, but this book is neither 'redoing' nor 'undoing'; my interest is rather in the 'doing' of feminism *in* digital media. As I argue throughout the book, *doing* feminism and *being* feminist involves enacting ourselves as activists – as embodied – and political subjects through media practices, technologies, the imaginaries linked to these new technologies and the internet.

There are a number of important questions that dim the optimism of digital feminism accounts. First of all, is it media technologies, old or new, digital or analogue, that are doing feminism (or redoing or undoing it)? Can we not detect in such a claim a cultural bias, in our 'culture of connectivity' (Van Dijck 2013), that places social media or otherwise visible-on-the-screen networks as the vanguard of feminist political action? Because of their celebration of the technological rather than the social, accounts of digital feminism largely disregard questions of cultural specificity and do not allow an investigation of agency in the multiple sites where it develops and gets expressed. But the relationship between media institutions and social life is dialectic and complex rather than causal, as it is captivated by the concept of mediation (Couldry 2008; Silverstone 2002). Mediation is

> the fundamentally, but unevenly, dialectical process in which institutiona-lized media of communication (the press, broadcast radio and television, and increasingly the world wide web), are involved in the general circulation of symbols in social life. (Silverstone 2002: 762)

Feminism is not merely a matter of representation, as I explain in the next section, but is enacted through these mediation processes.

Another key critique here is the reduction of the political to the personal and individual, which has been raised both by Lisa Duggan (2002) in relation to lesbian, gay, bisexual and transgender (LGBT) politics and by Angela Mcrobbie (2007) in relation to feminism. Choice and empowerment through consumerist practices are key discourses that circulate in popular media, and actively undermine the important gains of feminist and identity politics of 1970s and 1980s (Mcrobbie 2007). It is well documented that neoliberalism works by promoting self-management, self-monitoring, empowerment and individualism. These are the discourses that circulate in mainstream media, even for feminist events such as SlutWalk. Karen Darmon (2014) analysed the framing of SlutWalk in both online blogs written by feminists and in mainstream media news reporting, and saw that, indeed, post-feminist neoliberal discourses profoundly guide how the word 'slut' is translated in mainstream press. It is not surprising then that Darmon problematises how far the work that feminist activist cultures do to reclaim the word 'slut' actually benefits from the use of social media, if mainstream media continuously anchor feminist identity back to neoliberal discourses of femininity. This is namely as bodily property, as individualism, choice and empowerment (including self-surveillance, monitoring and discipline) (Gill 2007). Similar scepticism is expressed in a recent study of how, in digitally emerging countries such as India, for a successful feminist campaign (e.g. #victimblaming), hashtagging is only effective when it is combined with mainstream news media (Guha 2015).[3] This shows the difficulty in understanding what digital protest and media technologies mean for local cultures. The problematic relationship between mainstream media and local or marginalised activist cultures and social movements is perhaps only slightly eased with digital media technologies.

On a more moderate side of the debate are accounts of contemporary feminism and digital media that have used resource mobilisation theories[4] to stress how social media have enabled the speedy dissemination of information across borders, and have helped feminist organisations to form transnational networks. For example, Hande Elsen-Ziya writing recently about Turkish feminism traced how in the second decade of the 2000s, women's organisations moved from traditional media forms, such as leaflets, posters and faxes, to social networks, which 'gave speed and force' to their lobbying efforts (2013: 868). This is something that also stood out in participant accounts in my research on women's organisations based in London (Chapter 2). Among the participants in my study at a time of transition to new resources for political expression and lobbying, it was accepted that some form of digital connectivity was necessary in a competitive media environment. First, women's organisations have to compete with established structures of institutional power, for instance, by responding to governmental consultations, where agenda issues are already defined by powerful actors; second, they had to compete for political voice, recognition and publicity in online spaces where other social actors campaign. They were thus deeply concerned about their role and their capacity as situated political subjects, when the default mode of campaigning and communication for activists seemed to have become digital and networked. One important finding in this chapter is that technological imaginaries of horizontality and networked connectivity shape feminist activist cultures. Although hacking and self-empowerment through technologies are key technological imaginaries that shape geeky feminist cultures of the internet, these are strong visions of the internet for less tech-savvy feminist cultures. This case sets the tone of the book and some of the key questions for me here. How does our understanding of doing feminism and being feminist, and ultimately of being political, change in the digital age?

Embodiment, Labour and Practice

Early feminist theoretical engagement with network culture focused on identity experimentation and fluidity, but mostly overlooked how *collective* political identity develops (see Plant 1997; Stone 1995; Turkle 1996; Wakeford 1997). Meanwhile, research on social movements has been completely oblivious of gender and sexuality as sites of political struggle.[5] Media theorists examining the impact of digital networks on social movements have predominately looked for evidence of new public spheres, for example by looking at alternative media forms, such as Indymedia, anti-globalisation activism and online counterpublics (Atton 2002; Downing 2001; Papacharissi 2002; Ruiz 2014), or new media and citizen journalism (Gordon 2007; Dickens et al. 2014). Although this influential work offers vital insights into the transformation of publics and the opportunities for direct democracy, accounts about the embodied and social aspects of these publics remain underdeveloped. As a result, gender and sexuality, as embodied practices, have been invisible in both research about communication systems and studies of collective action, despite their centrality.

Yet we need to account for bodies and practices when thinking about feminist and queer politics, digital media and activism, not least because this is the site of immaterial or affective labour. Women have traditionally been assigned the role of caring, and despite important critiques of affective labour and digital media (see Hardt and Negri 2000; Fortunati 2007; Jarrett 2016), they still seem to be in contemporary seemingly leaderless social movements such as Occupy. In social media, women contribute what has been described as 'connective labour' in order to sustain the movement (Boler et al. 2014).[6] What is particularly problematic in this reflection is how, although second-wave feminism has been acknowledged as a historical influence for contemporary social movements, key gender issues and feminist vocabulary (such as 'patriarchy') seldom cross over, and gender equality is never raised as a central issue for social justice. Part of the problem is how, in the era of post-feminism and feminist backlash, feminism is assumed to have met its aims and to have gone past a stage of popularity; in other words, a 'pastness of feminism' is presupposed (Cohn 2013: 153). As digital media users are engaged in unpaid consumer labour in their everyday lives while social media platforms profiteer by harvesting their data, key questions of exploitation arise (see Fuchs 2014; Jarrett 2016).[7]

This invisible yet embodied labour in both everyday media and activist practices is part of the paradoxical aspect of digital media. Although in this book my interest is with the labour of producing activist media content *by feminists and queer activists for feminists and queer activists*, the implications of producing free labour are still relevant. I will explore this and other paradoxical characteristics and the usefulness of labour as an analytical tool in two chapters: the case of postporn cultures and online content production (Chapter 4) and the example of reproductive labour and transnational feminist networks (Chapter 3).

Labour is not the only aspect of materiality in relation to the digital that I am interested in this book. The concept of practice is also central for me here: the very conditions of political organising, and how we understand what it means to be political as feminists, are inextricably linked to communicative practices in network digital culture. In her analysis, Alice Mattoni (2012) draws primarily from Nick Couldry's (2004) theorisation of media practice, and from the work of John Postill (2009), to define activist media practices as, first, the knowledge-making practices and learning spaces for media production, and second, those practices that redefine the relationships of activists (as individuals and as groups) to mainstream media. Taking practice theory and citizen media a step further, in an exploration of the World Social Forum, Hilde Stephansen (2016) argues that citizen media practices do not just publicise issues and matters of concern. They also empower citizens to collaborate and form 'thick' social bonds and networks of solidarity across national borders, which allow them to formulate and disseminate their ideas and versions of social reality. What is important about Stephansen's provocation is the emphasis on the social significance of media practices that are at the same time pedagogical and political. Similarly to what we have explored elsewhere (Fotopoulou and Couldry 2015; Stephansen and Couldry 2014; Couldry et al. 2016), activists learn to use digital media technologies in informal networks. What is more,

> adopting a practice-oriented perspective involves rethinking the concept of (counter) publics, focusing on how citizen media practices can contribute not only to making public previously unreported issues and perspectives, but to the making of publics. A practice framework – by highlighting the material, embodied and social aspects of processes of public-formation – exposes the limitations of perspectives that see publics as constituted purely through the circulation of discourse. (Stephansen 2016: 38)

Although not strictly about citizen media, this book is about activist practices, both digital media based and more traditional forms of community building and identity formation. This combination is particularly illustrated in relation to queer activist cultures based in Brighton (Chapter 5) where the circulation and generation of activist media texts, such as printed fanzines and Facebook photographs of meetings and parties, make it possible for those who participate to build a safe community and to sustain a local social space. What is central here is that the mixture of digital media practices (such as wikis and corporate social networking platforms) with physical do-it-yourself (DIY) spaces do not just facilitate cultural meaning-making by sharing ideas and information; as I argue, these practices constitute a project of social world-making that is vital for queer politics. Activists see these spaces and technologies as pedagogic and as opportunities for learning how to live and how to be political. In this example, and also in the cases of London feminists (Chapter 2) and postporn networks (Chapter 4), digital media bring activists together in shared spaces to learn and experiment not only with technologies, but also with concepts and ideas, and serve as opportunities for forming networks, community and political subjectivity. An exploration of activist media practices in these examples involves both the symbolic and the material: the formation of collective identity and projects of symbolic world-making on the one hand; and on the other, all the material processes of setting up infrastructures and maintaining them in terms of technical expertise.

MATERIALITY AND REPRESENTATION

Now let me outline my more general approach to the question of materiality in this book, which informs the focus on the material, social and embodied aspects of digital media technologies and activist practices. There are different routes to get to the question of materiality, and different disciplines have historically been interested in matter for different reasons. Within feminist theory, which is relevant for me, and especially since the second-wave movement, the distinction between political or ideological representation and materiality has received significant attention; this has primarily manifested as a debate around the sex/gender dichotomy (Colebrook 2000: 77). Gender representation and the state of woman as 'other' in media and cultural texts (including science fiction, science communication and news media) has been a central concern in feminist media studies (see Braidotti 2002; Creed 1993). Although these interrogations are significant and provide a rich ground for debate regarding how women feature in political imaginaries, the question of cultural representation is also problematic because it positions women as passive victims of male-owned production, making the production of counter-representations the primary task for feminists (Bray and Colebrook 1998). It is not surprising, then, that recent interventions of material feminisms (Alaimo and Hekman 2008) move once again towards the question of materiality, aiming to place it at the centre of feminist philosophy. Meanwhile, representationalism has also been challenged by writers in political science and media theory focusing on the political possibilities offered in informational and networked environments. Let me highlight the ideas offered in these two strands of thought: first, I will look at the work of Tiziana Terranova (2004) and Jodie Dean (2009), both of whom in different ways challenge representationalism by orienting to the political; then, I will move on to examine 'posthumanist performativity' (Barad 2007) as a way of thinking about embodiment in digital networks beyond the matter/representation binary.

There are other scholars than Terranova to explore the limitations of representational approaches, but it is Terranova who has identified the 'divergence between a representational and an informational space' (2004: 36) that network connectivity carries. Terranova (2004) builds her framework on both Kittler's media environment theory and the theory of cybernetics and communication (developed by Claude E. Shannon, Norbert Weiner and John von Neumann) to propose a series of affirmative positions about cultural politics in informational milieus (Terranova 2004: 8). Terranova's aphorism that we need to 'move away from an exclusive focus on meaning and representation as the only political dimension in culture' (Terranova 2004: 9) is an important call to action. For me, taking on-board this prompt means that I have attended to the open-ended informational and social relationships developing within and between various groups and individuals, and second, that I have adopted mapping as a methodological attitude.[8] In addition to an analysis of representational politics and ideological positions, this book foregrounds the connections and encounters between actors, and their media practices, which I consider to be part of the affirmative and productive aspect of informational milieus. As I suggest in this book with a number of examples, it is these encounters and social relationships that present political potential in the digital spaces of informational flows. But older media forms remain powerful and find their way to us through digital media – precisely because older ways of experiencing the world are still important.

In the same vein as Terranova's position on network culture, other post-representational analyses have foregrounded the potential of social relationships and experimentation in forms of organising (e.g. Juris 2005; Milioni 2009). These studies have variably engaged with the idea of the 'multitude' to describe collective bodies – a model developed by Michael Hardt and Antonio Negri (2005). The multitude delineates multiple, distinct struggles, like short-lived assemblages around single issues, which gather together actors from diverse political positions and nations, and are non-hierarchically linked (2000: 103). In their influential work *Empire*, Hardt and Negri (2000) engage with the work of Gilles Deleuze and Felix Guattari, and Foucault, to theorise resistance as potentially present anywhere and everywhere, in 'a new context, a new milieu of maximum plurality and uncontainable singularization – a milieu of the event' (p. 25). Resistance is thus within labour for Hardt and Negri; it is in the new subjectivities offered in the 'living labor in contemporary capitalist society' (Hardt and Negri 2000: 29), which has both revolutionary and exploitative potential. This is clearly a Foucauldian reading of power as immanent: productive rather than repressive. Nonetheless, although Hardt and Negri's attention is with post-representational politics, potentially happening in all parts of our everyday lives and in all sites of the social, their gender-blindness makes their philosophy difficult to apply within a situated analysis of embodied gendered subjects.

Of course, feminist philosophers, who have approached questions of the body in non-representational ways (Braidotti 2002; Colebrook 2000, 2008; Grosz 1994) and found appeal in the work of Deleuze and Guattari, have done so with the purpose of offering feminism 'the possibility of a positive, active and affirmative ethics' (Bray and Colebrook 1998: 36). They have thus moved beyond Lacanian negation, in which the feminine is defined as lack or 'other' of the masculine order, and have formulated discourse as a bodily expression. In applying Deleuze's concepts of intensity, flow and machine to the example of anorexia for instance, Abigail Bray and Claire Colebrook (1998) interpret dietetic practices like weighing as modes of positive self-production of difference. Similarly, Braidotti's philosophical nomadism suggests an 'ethics of mutual interdependence' (2002: 226) in which biopolitical ethics are more important than identity politics as we know them. Indeed, we need to recognise the multiple differences in contemporary feminist and queer politics by attending to the different scales at which these struggles operate, as well as consider the sets of communicative practices that different actors adopt in their 'becoming' political. But, although I see the necessity of inventing new ways of thinking about politics in post-representational ways and in ways that bring Foucauldian understandings of biopower (or regimes that manage life) to contemporary technological environments, my thinking about biopolitics is different.

Today, being/living as a body is increasingly mediated by pornography, by internet memes, selfies and hashtags, by technoscience, medicine and celebrity culture. This process of mediation is ongoing and unfinished, shaped by non-human environments and contexts. Feminism, with its calls to seize the means of reproduction, to control one's body, to situate bodies and practices intersectionally, is a quintessentially biopolitical project (Murphy 2012: 10). As Michelle Murphy argues, bodies, flesh, suffering, pleasure and life are at the centre of feminist politics, and this focus has also signalled the significance of sex to contemporary forms of govern mentality. The acceleration of digital and biotechnological innovation and the dense connectedness that characterises our lives are today shaping such forms of governmentality, by changing the very material conditions in which life takes place. In this book, I account for how feminism and queer critique challenge these new forms of governmentality, while their political project is performed within digital capitalism. These, I argue, are inherently contradictory conditions for a biopolitical project. My focus on corporeal vulnerability, as an enabling rather than limiting element for politics, aims to tackle such contradiction and paradox.

This is also how I diverge from certain critiques of immanent power and politics. One such major critique (on the other side of the representational–informational friction that I outlined above) comes from Ernesto Laclau (2001) in a critique of *Empire*. Laclau argues that representation remains the central process for politicisation. The multiple positions, he writes, produced in informational and networked environments are not inherently political, as Hardt and Negri suggest. Laclau's insight is important here precisely because of the challenges of constructing a 'we' of strategic difference in new informational and communicative environments. Indeed, what remains unspecified in immanence approaches to network technologies and culture are the practical realities and pragmatic aspects of articulating collective political responses and, more crucially, what difference gender and sexuality make in these actions. In other words, the question of different bodies and different identities requiring different struggles keeps returning, perhaps with even more urgency. But once the notion of politics is re-oriented biopolitically towards shared conditions of corporeality in post-industrial worlds, as we will see, new understandings for non-oppositional politics are possible.

Another important critique of immanent politics and digital media comes from Jodi Dean, particularly in *Democracy and Other Neoliberal Fantasies* (2009). In contrast to what Terranova (2004) and Hardt and Negri (2000) understand as a space of potentiality, Dean's grim account describes a space of fragmentation and lost political causes. The volume of communicative content that disperses political struggles into a 'myriad of minor issues and events' (2009: 24) is for Dean not just problematic, but essentially depoliticising. While institutional politics continue no-matter-what, activists, contends Dean, 'struggle for visibility, currency, and in the now quaint term from dot-com years, mindshare' (2009: 20). For Dean, instead of resulting in heterogeneity, this productivity occludes antagonism between various political actors and eventually hinders political action – especially that coming from the left. It is essential to ask critical questions about the volume of activist media products and about the desire to participate and to interact in a book about feminist activism and digital media, although I reach somewhat different conclusions to Dean, as I explain below. A key critical point here is the role of abundance and productivity for the thriving of capitalism as a whole. 'Communicative capitalism', Dean poignantly argues, is in essence a free market achievement, which incorporates democratic aspirations – those of the 'active, emancipation-hungry consumer' (Frank cited in Dean 2009: 9).[9] Dean is right to argue that

> rhetorics of access, participation, and democracy work ideologically to secure the technological infrastructure of neoliberalism, an invidious and predatory politico-economic project that concentrates assets and power in the hands of the very, very rich, devastating the planet and destroying the lives of billions of people. (2009: 23)

Indeed, as my empirical research shows, women's and queer groups re-organise according to what they see as the demands of network conditions in the digital era and, for many, the struggle for representational space in networked environments can be seen as merely a quest for popularity. For example, in my examination of London feminist networks (Chapter 2), this struggle sometimes involves a project of symbolic annihilation of other political voices, like those of sex work activists, perhaps more than it signifies an alliance-building project. In other cases, for instance in relation to feminist porn production (Chapter 3) and feminist networks organising around reproductive technologies (Chapter 4), the impact of neoliberal entrepreneurship is evident in online political discourse.[10] In Chapter 3 in particular, we will see how commercial feminist porn integrates queer politics into branded sexualities and, subsequently, transforms political values into commercial value. This is a process of mediation that is essentially a process of value creation, whereby symbolic content gets exchange value and use value beyond their initial cultural value (see Lash and Lury 2007). Moreover, in these two examples, scarcity and abundance are useful concepts for understanding how the global and uneven traffic of bits of women's bodies and information is regulated.

However, the increasing phenomena of LGBT mainstreaming and consumerism (Chapter 5), the emergence of sexual politics bloggers (Chapter 4) and post-feminist consumer identities related to reproductive technologies (Chapter 3) do not, in my understanding, necessarily signify the end of politics, or, as Dean would have it, the failure to act or to elicit political responses (2009: 29). We need to be careful not to re-inscribe binaries between discourse and materiality, logos and action in digital media. We cannot simply frame politics as action and reduce digital communication to an exchange of encoded logical messages between civil society actors and the government. In other words, the assumption operating here is that because the internet is all about abundance of information and user-generated content, activism and politics are necessarily locked within a causal relationship with this information glut, as Andrejevic (2013) calls it. But doing politics – doing feminism – in digital media is not just about generating and circulating content, messages, images, bits, data and metadata. It is, as I noted earlier drawing from Stephansen (2016), about social processes of community formation and transformation of subjectivity, enabled by digital media practices. Historically, the focus on the semantic side – the rational side – has overshadowed the embodied aspect of political voice (Cavarero 2005). But democratic progressive politics, which includes feminist and queer politics, is a matter of articulating passions and extends to all sites of social life, as Chantal Mouffe (2005) has argued. For Mouffe, the task is to mobilise these passions and give them democratic outlet (1993:109). Natalie Fenton (2016) also reminds us that the 'politics of being' are characterised by passion, anger and hope, which need to be accounted for when studying digital media and radical politics. But the figure of the feminist has historically always been passionate and angry, seen in need of taming and rationality, from the Suffragette who furiously shakes her legs in the air, to the Women's Lib hippy who publicly burns her bra. The inability of liberal politics to encompass political passions relies partly on the attempt at 'domesticating hostility' (Mouffe 2005: 108), of persisting to reinstate conditions of rational harmony. In this book, hope about digital networks and feminism, anxiety about the commodification of women's tissue and other bodily material, anger about the commercialisation of gay Pride and the experience of viewing a pornographic film are all examples of embodied and medium-specific conditions in which affective relations and passionate politics emerge in digital media today. As I explain with these illustrations, feminist and queer activist formations appear around issues, events and practices, both at street level and in transient online public spaces. Therefore, shifting the emphasis away from debates about the failure of democratic politics and digital networked capitalism that mainly focus on scarcity and abundance of information and data in the digital era to include affect, embodiment and sociality helps me reach my particular interest in biopolitics and global governmentality.

BIODIGITAL VULNERABILITY

From this interest in biopolitics, and my understanding of feminism as a historically biopolitical project that *does* as well as evaluates technoscience (Murphy 2012), it is necessary to introduce another central dimension that links activism, digital media and embodiment in this book (in addition to the important focus on practices): that of vulnerability as a pre-condition for enabling feminist and queer political subjectivity. I use here Judith Butler's discussion on violence, mourning and feminist politics (2004), which is concerned precisely with the materialisation of embodied publics, alliances and other political relationships. She writes:

> each of us is constituted politically in part by virtue of the social vulnerability of our bodies – as a site of desire and physical vulnerability, as a site of publicity at once assertive and exposed. Loss and vulnerability seem to follow from our being socially constituted bodies, attached to others, at risk of losing those attachments, exposed to others, at risk of violence by virtue of that exposure. (2004: 20)

Butler's argument has a great asset: unlike any other account, it makes the public recognition of corporeal common vulnerability a pre-condition for articulating ethical, political claims. Our own bodies, she writes, have a public dimension and are constituted as a 'public phenomenon' (Butler 2004: 26) and it is because of this that it is possible to imagine community and politics. Why is this useful in a book about feminism and digital media? Vulnerability has been a stumbling block for feminism because of its connotations with passivity and victimisation. But consider how feminism against rape culture (sexual violence, street harassment and misogyny in the everyday life of girls and women, especially on campuses) has transformed with social media. Today, the popularity of Twitter and other microblogging social media platforms offer great opportunities for articulating responses to rape culture. 'Hashtag feminism' as it is often called, allows feminist to challenge representations of sexual violence and discourses around rape in music and popular culture. Examples of hashtag activism such as #AskThicke and #safetytipsforladies, and many others, expose victim blaming and the shaming of women in social networks, often by using humour as a political tool for building resilience (see Horeck 2014; Loza 2014; Rentschler 2014, 2015). But there is another significant aspect in this form of feminist activism that has to do with affect and temporality of digital media:

> There is now an unprecedented speed and immediacy to affective responses to rape and its hyper visible circulation online; it is the radical potentialities and limitations of this new temporal regime – epitomized by the hashtag – that we as feminists must consider when strategizing how to actively re-shape the cultural consensus on questions of gender, violence and power. (Horeck 2014: 1106)

Immediacy, as a key characteristic of digital media, and the bias towards the new temporalities it enables are however in this book raised as a 'sticky' point. This is because in many examples presented in this book, the everyday experiences of doing activism is far from immediate; meetings and parties are long, and process is essential for formulating voice for feminists and queer activists in this study.[11] According to Jay David Bolter and Richard Grusin's (1999) model of remediation, immediacy however also refers to the logic of making the medium disappear so that the experience from one setting or reality to another appears unmediated.[12] But as this book shows, the media are constant material agents of politicisation and digital networks are essential in imagining and enacting feminist and queer subjectivity. Thinking about the different overlapping temporalities, those defined by historical traces to the past, those of the new and immediate and those of the slow and long-lasting of everyday processes, through the different empirical examples that the book presents, helps us not only maintain the media visible, but also understand how feminism and queer activism operate in multi-layered networks and relationships across time, scales and technologies.

In addition to the changing understandings of vulnerability that the example of hashtag feminism against rape culture offers however, there is another reason to rethink vulnerability as a productive concept when it comes to digital media. Recently the affective turn in queer cultural theory has recognised the political potential of negative emotions and experiences. Particularly, the work of Sarah Ahmed, Heather Love and Sally Munt has reframed queer as a shameful identity and offers a fundamental insight into the historical importance of gay stigma for contemporary identity. In *Queer Attachments: The Cultural Politics of Shame*, Sally Munt (1998) argues that shame is not necessarily a negative feeling; its political potential has led to collective action, claims for recognition, political presence and legitimation and has been proven historically with the examples of the Black Civil Rights movement, Gay Liberation Front and Women's Liberation. Shame is embodied and inscribed in our bodies – especially when the body is the source of shame, for example when there is disfigurement, or any other shame of 'non-conformity'. Meanwhile, as Munt notes, shame does not only operate on an individual level, but it also operates at a national level; think, for example, how Germany and Japan were committed to a post-World War II project of national reconstruction and rebuilding of their national identity. Indeed, shame can lead to 'radical, instigating, social, political and cultural agency amongst the formerly dis-enfranchised' (Munt 1998: 3). Ahmed (2002) also sees emotions as central to politics, because of the attachments and investments required in order for people to become subject of power. If we think about how a range of negative feelings, including regret, despair, self-hatred and loneliness, can result from mediation, for example from the circulation of negative toxic and tragic messages about same-sex desire in film, pop culture and digital cultures, it become even clearer how the embodied and affective, the political and the personal, overlap. Heather Love in *Feeling Backwards* (2009) suggests that the media texts that inspire such feelings are tied to the experience of social exclusion and the impossibility of same sex desire, which is why they can have such much more intense effects than when we watch relatively positive representations. Recognising this link publicly can be immensely empowering.

Consider also how affect and social relations are becoming central in social media data mining for predictive analytics and marketing (Kennedy 2016; Andrejevic 2013). As Ingrid Volkmer (2014) has argued, global communicative spheres and networks are no longer just digital; they are beyond social communities of friends. 'They have become platforms for subjectively "lived" public spaces' (2014: 1) that challenge our very understanding of media and civic identity. And as we are moving to an era of the Internet of Things, where our phones, our cars and domestic appliances are connected, 'we not only do things with words but also do words with things' (Isin and Ruppert 2015: 2). Isin and Ruppert explain that connectivity has not only transformed the ways we live, but because of the connective webs between things and people, and the increasing reliance of public authorities on these webs for data collection, it is transforming politics. Meanwhile, today new media technologies and digital culture, alongside biological technologies, constitute a historically specific set of regulatory practices, discourses and institutions but also forms of participation; this is what Haraway (1997), by appropriating Foucault's (1978) biopower, called 'technobiopower'. This means that new kinds of vulnerability are generated. Culture in global information networks is indeed biotechnological (Kember 2003). I prefer the term 'biodigital', not so much to point out the integration of information and biotechnologies in both culture and science (O'riordan 2010), but rather to focus on the lived, embodied and experienced aspects of the digital, in the coming together of *bios* (life) and the digital. Butler's argument, alongside a consideration of affect, is especially valuable because it allows us to consider how digital (and biological) technological acceleration constitute today new forms of governmentality, and how these paradoxically can offer possibilities for articulating new political subjectivities.

Life with digital media technologies results in certain distinct vulnerabilities for women and queer people. I noted earlier the invisibility of embodied and affective labour specifically by women in relation to the material media practices in social media and activism. We can also think about the increased expectations for visibility for teenage girls, women, trans and queer youth who are claiming a voice in a culture where they risk being the target of misogynistic trolling and gay cyberbullying. The supposed shift of power to the user in the digital era comes hand-in-hand with the inevitable vulnerability of exposure, and as Andrejevic (2009) argues, the naturalisation of surveillance as we learn to watch and be watched. Recognising these new types of biodigital vulnerabilities publicly has been politically enabling for many feminist groups recently as I explain by drawing on many examples – from the cases of queer teenage suicides linked to cyber bullying, to the vilification and monitoring of teenage girls who engage in sexting, and the marginalisation of women in geeky technological cultures. Today many geeky feminists cultures, for example feminist hacking spaces and Quantified Self[13] women-only meetups, which I discuss in Chapter 4, have moved beyond plain questions of online access to issues and negotiations of visibility of difference. Feminist hacking spaces in particular are concerned with redefining the presence and visibility of marginalised groups in technology production (Fox et al. 2015). We may also note the harassment of women in the gaming culture, and the feminist organising around the Gamergate controversy.[14] In this case, geek masculinity merged with anti-feminist discourse to create a 'toxic technoculture' on the community site Reddit.com (Massanari 2015). Trolling and rape threats on social media define public life in conditions of biodigital vulnerability for these women and feminist cultures because they introduce new forms of control, not only of bodies and their movements, but also the circulation of discourse and their production of knowledge. In response, these cultures organise politically or form political subjectivities of marginalisation and increasingly turn to creating feminist spaces of mutual awareness and cooperation.[15] This is not to say that vulnerability and corporeal risk are inherently political. Instead, I suggest that the conscious practice of making the vulnerability public by placing it into its sociopolitical and historical context, a process that feminist and queer activists have historically undertaken, drains these conditions of their harmfulness and can be empowering.

A MORE PHILOSOPHICAL DISCUSSION: POSTHUMANIST PERFORMATIVITY

Beyond thinking about the circulation of communicative messages and representation vs. practice, and how central these are for the formation of feminist political subjectivity and queer identity, there are other significant questions to be asked at a deeper philosophical level. How do digital media technologies contribute to the creation of new material realities for feminist and queer activists? Are digital media just things, or can we attribute some kind of agency to them? And how are matter, knowledge, politics and subjects produced in digital media? One obvious way to approach such questions is via political economy. But my focus on the social, embodied and material aspects of digital media technologies and feminist activism has also been informed at a conceptual level by contemporary feminist scholars in science, technology, society (STS) and the contemporary scholarly field of material feminism, which address questions of the political in new technoscientific worlds (see Alaimo and Hekman 2008).

These take a different route to the question of technology and social equality: they concentrate on technoscientific practices and technologies that produce knowledge. Attending to the productivity of discursive practices, work in this strand indicates how practices, like those taking place in the microcosm of the lab, produce different versions of reality (see Barad 2007; Law and Mol 2002; Lawrence and Shapin 1998; Thompson 2005). So when Donna Haraway (1997) talks about discourse, she includes all the material/semiotic arrangements and practices that make up an object of knowledge – for example a cell or gene. Although in these studies the focus remains with discourse, technologies of knowledge making, and the ways in which observational media construct what they aim to describe, they variously engage with the question of power, resistance and biopolitical life. But how can we apply this framework to digital communication technologies and the ways they create socio-political structures and material realities?

As noted, studies focusing on feminism and digital media often neglect the materiality of the media and the versatile roles that they fulfil in the everyday lives of activists. But the media, either new or with the incorporation of older media forms, are constant material agents in the process of politicisation. This is a good reason to re-orient our attention towards a version of mediation in which the medium is present as materiality, as apparatus. As recent media ecology approaches have noted, 'technology is not only a passive surface for the inscription of meanings and signification, but a material assemblage that partakes in machinic ecologies' (Goddard and Parikka 2011: 1). What the media do and how they change in their materiality as technoscientific objects is important but we must be careful not to perceive them as 'things'. In feminist STS scholarship, this concern is particularly emphasised by Karen Barad (2007) in *Meeting the Universe Halfway*, where she brings together Michel Foucault's theorisation of discursive practices and the ideas of quantum physicist Neils Bohr, to develop the concept of 'posthumanist performativity'. Barad is uneasy with both Butler's notion of performativity and Foucault's discursive practices in relation to the production of material bodies and directs her emphasis to the agency of non-humans. Focusing specifically on the materiality of scientific apparatuses and technologies of knowing, Barad (2003) questions the attention that human discourse and language has received by post-structuralist thinkers and increasingly by feminist STS scholars. She frames discursive practices or apparatus as non-human-based practices that in their own right produce local and physical conditions. For instance, in an analysis of how the scanning tunnelling microscope was used to create the IBM logo on a subatomic level, Barad (2007:354–364) traces the making of new materialities and a new kind of expert (the nanotechnologist). In an earlier study, she analysed how the sonogram, a technology used to follow the progress of a human pregnancy, gave a new status to both the foetus and the politics of life (Barad 1998). In these studies, Barad is not interested in the meanings and cultural ideas around technoscientific practices, but rather in the material/semiotic effects that these have, the realities that they performatively produce and their socio-political implications.

While Barad's concern is with phenomena happening on a smaller scale (that of the lab) than those I analyse in this book, her insights about non-human agency enable the possibility of thinking about digital media and network communication technologies in a way that does not instrumentalise them. Digital media, including screens, cables and keyboards; smartphones and GPS devices; online financial transactions, file sharing and virtual credit; social networking and digitisation of archives; digital research methods and databases of visualisations, can all be seen as discursive practices that produce socio-political realities. It is through our use, engagement and entanglement with these technologies that we become feminists and perform feminism. As I have argued, this performance is not just a matter of words and discourse, it is an embodied practice; it is the things we do online. My focus on how we enact ourselves as feminists through these connective technologies, while at the same time, we create digital networks. This approach does not pre-suppose that a particular feminist subjectivity and activist practice, existing in physical social spaces and on the streets, is then merely juxtaposed on a digital environment. As is the case with Gerbaudo's (2012) analysis in *Tweets and the Streets*, social actors form and act in physical spaces and through their use of social media and other platforms. Posthumanist performativity above all stresses the importance of process. This makes Barad's theoretical contribution indispensable for a reconsideration of the reciprocity between culture and technology and informs my theorisation of how subjects and objects emerge in digital networks.

Notes on Methods

My research design involved engaging in activities with various organisations, groups and individuals in both online and offline contexts. My choice of case studies was motivated as much by my desire to better understand key aspects of digital networks (access, connectivity, immediacy, labour and visibility), as by the need to account for themes central in feminist and queer politics (bodily autonomy, pornography, reproduction and quality of social life). Conducting in-depth interviews, going to parties and agenda-setting meetings and tracing the connections and journeys of feminist and queer formations online and offline allowed me to understand the complex processes of building individual and collective identity and online presence; and the processes of negotiation of digital technologies. These processes were shaped by the intersecting categories of oppression for the participants of this study, like class, sexuality, ethnicity and gender, and by the more general socio-cultural context of the post-2008 economic recession where my research took place. Further inspired by intersectionality studies (Anthias and Yuval-Davis 1983; Collins 2000; Crenshaw 1989; Davis 2008; Erel 2007; Fotopoulou 2012; Mccall 2005; Mohanty 1988; 2003), I attempt a self-critical production of knowledge, by registering my own intersectional location throughout. This is necessary precisely because, by moving through both online and offline spaces as a researcher in each of the cases examined in the chapters of this book, I was also a user, a producer and consumer of digital media. This book should thus be seen as a production of embodied knowledge, reflective of my own position, as someone with intersecting identities, such as white and cis-woman.

One of these identities was that of a PhD student. As academic and activist spaces frequently crossed, I would meet in conferences people known to me from my fieldwork. These encounters were an important part of negotiating my own researcher and feminist identity through this project, as I attempted to differentiate my political opinion from the positions various feminist and queer groups articulated, whilst remaining supportive of their struggles. My other identity was my national identity, as a Greek living in the UK. When I started my fieldwork in 2009, the worldwide economic crisis was still unravelling, but had already released unprecedented economic and social misery in Greece and other under-privileged countries of the European Union. When Athens was burning in the 2008 riots, or when Syntagma Square signalled the promise of direct democracy once again, along with the Indignados and other mobilisations around Europe, the pain of *nostos* and the agony of not-belonging could not have been more intense. To add to the complexity, moving from a working class background to the environment of the academy, where everyone is imagined to be middle class almost magically, made my research journey an adventure – especially when I interviewed working class people. Then, being my working class self sometimes felt almost like passing, I just wasn't working class enough anymore. These overlapping identities, and the experience of being and doing feminism in digital networks, have made it clear to me how my account is partial, in that it does not claim to speak for the object of study; it is accountable, by registering my position as a researcher and sensitive to the vulnerability that the research account can generate. These three important steps follow Haraway's (1997) advice against 'reflexivity' and in favour of 'diffraction',

the optical metaphor that describes the research process as an attempt not to repeat something that is supposedly authentic, but to produce 'difference patterns in the worlds, not just the same reflected – displaced – elsewhere' (Haraway 1997: 268).[16]
Feminist and queer politics happen in different contexts; they take place online, offline and across different scales and overlapping layers. They are context- and medium-specific. To maintain this multiplicity of feminist and queer forms of activism, the way that I have written each chapter and the examples that illustrate my key arguments in this book are indeed topological,[17] in the sense that they attempt to conceive changeable and abstract objects and their connections (as is the case with politics in informational and networked spaces). This topological approach has also allowed me to account for the complex multi-layered relationships between different forms of feminism and queer activism and their histories, across time and space – sometimes antagonistic, sometimes supportive. Hence the three dimensions of this topology are 'how', 'what' and 'where'. We may think of the topological aspect of 'where' as something that describes dynamic locations, at the intersection of web and offline spaces, flows and scales. 'What' concerns the material/semantic form that feminist and queer activism takes in this context, such as the online content, but also imaginaries and metaphors. And 'how' relates to the processes and practices of emergence, such as online media as actor shaping political issues, everyday connections and mediated experiences.

ITINERARY

The book is organised as follows. Chapter 2 begins to investigate new activist media practices by drawing on ethnography with various feminist organisations and individuals based in London. I focus on how these actors understood the role of digital media in contemporary feminism. My fieldwork shows how activists negotiate access, connectivity, immediacy, labour and visibility, the key characteristics of digital technologies, while they raised important points of critique about technical expertise and unpaid labour in the context of post-2008 austerity. Of particular interest here is how activist practices are influenced by libertarian promises that make up a shared social imaginary of the internet as an empowering technology. There is a wider rhetoric of digital networks as sites of non-hierarchical modes of connection and as elementary components of democratic participation. My argument is that this imaginary influences what counts as legitimate political engagement for feminists today and is instrumental in shaping the form and agendas of women's organisations. The findings demonstrate that indeed, the internet presents an alternative way of engagement for many London-based women groups as it provides spaces for rapid circulation of their campaign material, and connection with one another. At the same time, it becomes a space where older feminists, who are not 'digital natives', experience an uncomfortable sense of being left behind and forgotten about. With this discussion, the chapter portrays how the web becomes a new mediated context of increased visibility and connectivity, part of the wider media ecology, where political opinions about old and still unresolved feminist issues are being reformulated whilst vulnerability and empowerment are experienced in new mediated ways.

In Chapter 3, I move on to examine the tensions and contradictions that characterise feminist and queer pornographic production and self-exposure practices in the era of 'selfie' culture. Here I begin to untangle some of the past and present feminist debates on pornography by addressing issues around web visibility and communication technology more generally, and by contextualising them in light of contemporary postporn politics. Moving away from questions of representation, my question is: what is political about these practices? My analysis first focuses on how postporn cultures raise critical questions about communicative capitalism, about what it means to be human and how we can live with digital technologies, and how they reflect on profound anxieties about what constitutes authenticity and individuality. Then I continue to explore two exemplary cases: nofauxxx.com, a queer and women-owned porn production company that claims a feminist identity; and Shu Lea Cheang's 2001 film *I.K.U.*, a Japanese sci-fi postporn/artporn film, and make special mention of explicit selfies and the so-called 'selfie feminism'. By employing a biopolitical framework of network capitalism, I offer a substantive account of the complex relationship between feminism and the online porn market, to show how queer and feminist identities are becoming increasingly diffused. Although scholarly work in queer and postporn studies has variously conceptualised bioart and sex-positive blogging as expressions of resistance to a normative sexual order, I argue that content generation by both artists and companies is largely guided by neoliberal discourses of consumer choice and sexual agency, in the same way as any other porn production without a specifically feminist or/and queer agenda. At the same time, producers of queer porn and participants in postporn networks are aware of their subordination and the new forms of biodigital vulnerability, which differentiates them significantly from heterosexual amateur porn cultures. It is because of this awareness and negotiations of vulnerability, I suggest, that the networked connections, events and practices of these actors can be politically empowering.

In Chapter 4, I revisit the concept of networked feminism within the wider context of debates in contemporary feminism about forms of gendered and reproductive labour (Dickenson 2007; Franklin and Lock 2003; Thompson 2005). I turn here to account for feminist projects of knowledge production about reproductive technologies and their regulation in digital media, focusing specifically on the example of fertility policy around egg donation and fertility tracking with smart technologies. The significance of reproductive labour for global capitalism, and the biodigital vulnerabilities that are created in relation to reproductive technologies are my key interests in this discussion. Reproductive labour and the changes in the political economy of reproduction brought by new reproductive technologies, such as in vitro fertilisation and egg extraction, are controversial issues that have invited numerous feminist interventions around the world. A conceptualisation of gendered labour is vital for an understanding of the reconfigurations of the 'political' in our digitally mediated worlds. Second, I move on to analyse the communicative acts that contribute to a layperson's knowledge production about reproductive rights, and note how these cut across academic/grassroots, online/offline and national/local spaces, whilst challenging these boundaries. Feminist networks attempt to create alternative but credible sources of knowledge that question dominant understandings of biomedicine and its policy. My examination shows how these actors establish their credibility and how their participation in mainstream digital media legitimises them as representatives of affected groups in society. The central pre-occupation with subjective experience and seizing control over one's body in contemporary feminist mobilisations indicates continuity with the Women's Health Movement. As with the other chapters in this book, there are deep contradictions that characterise feminist politics of reproduction, as neoliberal discourses of individual choice, sexual agency and empowerment shape the conditions in which they emerge. I argue that these politics can be better understood in relation to embodied, material practices of knowledge production, mutual learning and self-experimentation with digital media and smart technologies.

From the international biopolitical networks of reproduction and pornography, I cross over to consider the specificity and importance of locality and space for queer political cultures in digital networks in Chapter 5. I am motivated here by the need to understand how the meaning of belonging, community and politics are changing with digital networking technologies. I draw from ethnographic analysis of an anarcho-queer activist group in Brighton called Queer Mutiny, and examine how reterritorialisation and community building were key elements of their political project. Through a combination of pedagogic and cultural activist practices, where peer support and learning are central, activists built a strong sense of place, and maintained an active connection between the past, the present and the future. These practices involved workshops and parties, as well as the production of DIY zines and online content, and aimed at creating a community life with thick and strong ties. Through a discussion of the group's resistance to digital media technologies, I show how social networking was in this case key in a project of world-making, as a means for documenting and promoting assets of community and strengthening embodied affective relations on the ground. Meanwhile, the chapter shows the tensions between how participants imagined global activism and how this activism materialised locally, against this backdrop of neoliberalism and the 'pink pound'. With an attention to intimacy, friendship and belonging and their centrality for local political communities and cultures, the chapter returns to a key concern in this book: the ways in which, in the digital world, feminist and queer activism are today performed and enacted through affective relations and material, embodied practices.

A key focus in this book are the contradictions, tensions and often-paradoxical aspects of feminist and queer politics in a digital world of dense connections. How can feminism and queer activism articulate a political response to the new forms of governmentality that result from digital technologies, while using these same technologies in order to circulate their counter-narratives and inhabit their versions of the world? By crossing through the themes of bodily autonomy, pornography, reproduction and queer social life, I visit some of the inherent contradictions of this political project and stress that, between empowerment and vulnerability, feminism remains today a necessary and passionate struggle for social justice.

NOTES

1. 'Web 2.0' is a term used to describe contemporary convergence and it refers to wikis, social networking platforms, weblogs and other user-generated content platforms and practices.
2. Intersectionality is the systematic study of the ways in which differences such as race, gender, sexuality, class, ethnicity and other sociopolitical and cultural categories interrelate. See Fotopoulou (2012) for an overview.
3. Guha (2015) explains how the campaign hashtags never really took off, or as they say, trending, and this for them is indicative of how the campaign did not manage to engage concerned citizens and policymakers.
4. Resource mobilisation theory is a theory of collective action, which focuses on organisational dynamics and the importance of resources such as time, money, technical and organisational skills for social movements. It has been employed in order to understand the role of social networking and other digital media technologies as new resources for activism, not only in terms of organising protest, but also for collective identity formation and fostering community bonds. See Eltantawy and Wiest (2011).
5. There are a few notable exceptions, such as Touraine (1981) who wrote about the women's liberation movement as a new social movement.
6. The authors extend Bennett and Segerberg's (2012) notion of 'connective action' here.
7. As Gill and Pratt (2008) explain, precarious employment in neoliberalism has a double meaning: on the one hand, it creates uncertainty, and on the other, the potential for new subjectivities and political possibilities.
8. Mapping as a methodological approach is explained in the following section.
9. In a later analysis, Andrejevic (2013) also notes how the internet has been understood as an empowering technology precisely because of its capacity to allow information production and distribution.
10. For other important examples employing Foucault's [what?] (2003; 2008), see Gajjala et al. (2010); Shakhsari (2011).
11. See also Barassi (2015) and Kaun (2015) for a discussion of how this operates in other activist and protest contexts.
12. According to the theory of remediation, visual digital culture presents itself as an improved version of older media in an effort to respond to them. Remediation is a process in which new cultural and media forms carry in and with them conventions, practices and ways of thinking which belonged to older cultural forms. They call the encounter and collocation of multiple cultural texts within any given digital text 'hypermediacy', whereas by 'immediacy' they refer to the concurrent invisibility of the medium in these texts. See also Kember and Zylinska (2012).

13. The Quantified Self (QS) is a community of people who use wearable devices in order to log personal information and improve various aspects of personal life, such as mood, physical and mental performance, or other aspects of everyday life, such as air quality.

14. The Gamergate controversy relates to the misogynistic campaign that was launched with the Twitter hashtag #GamerGate and involved the direct targeting of game developers Zoë Quinn and Brianna Wu, as well as cultural critic Anita Sarkeesian. The case sparked a feminist response and examination of issues of sexism in the video game industry.

15. A good example here is how the 2014 YouTube video about a woman who got 'catcalled' 108 times while walking in New York went viral with 43 million views (10 hours of walking in NYC as a woman). Although not directly linked to gender, the use of mobile phone cameras to expose police brutality against black people in the USA is at the time of writing another illustration of how publicity can empower marginalised communities.

16. For Haraway (1988), one task is to reveal the claims of power concealed in claims for objectivity. Central in this ethical and political project, particularly through the 'modest witness' figure, was of course registering gender exclusions in the making of scientific knowledge (Haraway 1997).

17. Topology derives from Greek, where it means an account of a conceptual structure or space, or according to *The Oxford English Dictionary* (1989), it is simply 'the way in which constituent parts are interrelated or arranged'. However, as a distinct mathematical field that focuses on continuity between objects it has informed numerous studies in network architecture (Elahi and Elahi 2006; Naimzada et al. 2009), music (Mazzola et al. 2002) and art (Kalajdzievski 2008; Martinot 2001).

BIBLIOGRAPHY

Ahmed, S. (2002). Communities that feel: Intensity, difference and attachment. In E. Larreta (Ed.), *Identity and difference in the global era* (pp. 414–448). Rio de Janerio: UNESCO.

Alaimo, S., & Hekman, S. J. (2008). *Material feminisms.* Bloomington, IN: Indiana University Press.

Andrejevic, M. (2009). Exploiting YouTube: Contradictions of user-generated labor. *The YouTube Reader*, 413.

Andrejevic, M. (2013). *Infoglut: How too much information is changing the way we think and know.* London: Routledge.

Anthias, F., & Yuval-Davis, N. (1983). Contextualising feminism: Gender, ethnic and class divisions. *Feminist Review, 15*, 62–75.

Atton, C. (2002). *Alternative media.* London: SAGE.

Baer, H. (2015). Redoing feminism: Digital activism, body politics, and neoliberalism. *Feminist Media Studies*, 0777(January), 17–34.

Barad, K. (1998). Getting real: Technoscientific practices and the materialization of reality. *Differences: A Journal of Feminist Cultural Studies*, 10(2), 87–91.

Barad, K. M. (2003). Posthumanist performativity: Toward an understanding of how matter comes to matter. *Signs*, 28, 801–831.

Barad, K. M. (2007). *Meeting the universe halfway: Quantum physics and the entanglement of matter and meaning.* Durham, NC: Duke University Press.

Barassi, V. (2015). Social media, immediacy and the time for democracy: Critical reflections on social media as temporalizing practices. In L. Dencik & O. Leistert (Eds.), *Critical perspectives on social media and protest: Between control and emancipation.* London: Rowman & Littlefield.

Bennett, W. L., & Segerberg, A. (2012). *The logic of connective action: Digital media and the personalization of contentious politics.* Cambridge: Cambridge University Press.

Boler, M., et al. (2014). Connective labor and social media: Women's roles in the 'leaderless' occupy movement, *Convergence: The International Journal of Research into New Media Technologies.*

Bolter, D., & Grusin, J. (1999). *Remediation: Understanding new media.* Cambridge, MA: MIT Press.

Braidotti, R. (2002). *Metamorphoses: Towards a materialist theory of becoming.* Cambridge, UK: Polity Press in association with Blackwell Publishers.

Bray, A., & Colebrook, C. (1998). The haunted flesh: Corporeal feminism and the politics of (dis)embodiment. *Signs: Journal of Women in Culture and Society*, 24(1), 35–67.

Butler, J. (2004). *Precarious life: The powers of mourning and violence.* London: Verso.

Cavarero, A. (2005). *For more than one voice toward a philosophy of vocal expression.* Stanford: Stanford University Press.

Cochrane, K. (2013) The fourth wave of feminism: Meet the rebel women. *The Guardian*, December 10. http://www.theguardian.com/world/2013/dec/10/fourth-wave-feminism-rebel-women

Cohn, J. (2013). Female labor and digital media: Pattie Maes, postfeminism, and the birth of social networking technologies. *Camera Obscura*, 28(2), 151–176.

Colebrook, C. (2000). From radical representations to corporeal becomings: The feminist philosophy of Lloyd, Grosz, and Gatens. *Hypatia*, 15, 76–93.

Colebrook, C. (2008). On not becoming man: The materialist politics of unactualized potential. In S. Alaimo & S. J. Hekman (Eds.), *Material feminisms.* Bloomington, IN: Indiana University Press.

Collins, P. H. (2000). It's all in the family: Intersections of gender, race, and nation. In U. Narayan & S. Harding (Eds.), *Decentering the center: Philosophy for a multicultural, postcolonial, and feminist world.* Bloomington, IN: Indiana University Press.

Couldry, N. (2004). Theorising media as practice. *Social Semiotics, 14*(2), 115–132.

Couldry, N. (2008). Mediatization or mediation? Alternative understandings of the emergent space of digital storytelling. *New Media & Society, 10*, 373–391.

Couldry, N., Fotopoulou, A., & Dickens, L. (2016). Real social analytics: A contribution towards a phenomenology of a digital world. *British Journal of Sociology, 67*(1), 118–137.

Creed, B. (1993). *The monstrous-feminine: Film, feminism, psychoanalysis.* London: Routledge.

Crenshaw, K. (1989). Demarginalising the intersection of race and sex: A black feminist critique of antidiscrimination doctrine, feminist theory, and antiracist politics. *University of Chicago Legal Forum, 14*, 538–554.

Darmon, K. (2014). Framing SlutWalk London: How does the privilege of feminist activism in social media travel into the mass media?. *Feminist Media Studies, 14*(4), 700–704.

Davis, K. (2008). Intersectionality as buzzword. *Feminist Theory, 9*, 67–85.

Dean, J. (2009). *Democracy and other neoliberal fantasies: Communicative capitalism and left politics.* Durham, NC: Duke University Press.

Della Porta, D., & Mattoni, A. (2012). Cultures of participation in social movements. *The Participatory Cultures Handbook, 170*–181.

Dickens, L., Couldry, N., & Fotopoulou, A. (2014). News in the community? Investigating emerging inter-local spaces of news production/consumption. *Journalism Studies, 16*(1), 97–114.

Dickenson, D. (2007). *Property in the body: Feminist perspectives.* Cambridge: Cambridge University Press.

Downing, J. (2001). *Radical media: Rebellious communication and social movements.* California: Sage Publications.

Duggan, L. (2002). The new homonormativity: The sexual politics of neoliberalism. In R. Castronovo & D. D. Nelson (Eds.), *Materializing democracy: Toward a revitalized cultural politics.* Durham, NC: Duke University Press.

Elahi, A., & Elahi, M. (2006). *Data, network, and Internet communications technology.* Clifton Park, NY: Thomson Delmar Learning.

Elsen-Ziya, H. (2013). Social media and Turkish feminism: New resources for social activism. *Feminist Media Studies, 13*(5), 860–870.

Eltantawy, N., & Wiest, J. B. (2011). The Arab Spring|Social media in the Egyptian revolution: Reconsidering resource mobilization theory. *International Journal of Communication, 5*, 1207–1224.

Erel, U. (2007). Constructing meaningful lives: Biographical methods in research on migrant women *Sociological Research Online* 12.

Fenton, N. (2016). *Digital, political, radical.* Cambridge: Polity.

Fortunati, L. (2007). Immaterial labor and its machinization. *Ephemera, 7*, 139–157.

Fotopoulou, A., & Couldry, N. (2015). Telling the story of the stories: Online content curation and digital engagement. *Information, Communication & Society, 18*(2), 235–249.

Fotopoulou, A. (2012). Intersectionality queer studies and hybridity: Methodological frameworks for social research. *Journal of International Women's Studies, 13*(2), 19–32.

Foucault, M. (1978). *The history of sexuality. Vol. 1: The will to knowledge.* London: Penguin Books Ltd.

Foucault, M. (2003). *Society must be defended: Lectures at the Collège de France, 1975–76.* New York: Picador.

Foucault, M. (2008). *The birth of biopolitics: Lectures at the Collège de France, 1978–79.* Basingstoke: Palgrave Macmillan.

Fox, S., Ulgado, R. R., & Rosner, D. K., (2015) Hacking culture, not devices: Access and recognition in feminist hackerspaces. *ACM*, CSCW 15, 14–18 March 2015.

Franklin, S., & Lock, M. M. (2003). *Remaking life & death: Toward an anthropology of the biosciences.* Santa Fe: School of American Research Press.

Fuchs, C. (2014). *Digital labour and Karl Marx.* New York: Routledge.

Gajjala, R., Zhang, Y., & Dako-Gyeke, P. (2010). Lexicons of women's empowerment online. *Feminist Media Studies, 10,* 1.

Galloway, A. R. (2004). *Protocol: How control exists after decentralization.* Cambridge, MA: MIT Press.

Gerbaudo, P. (2012). *Tweets and the streets: Social media and contemporary activism.* London: Pluto Press.

Gill, R. (2001). *Gender and the media.* Cambridge: Polity.

Gill, R. (2007). *Gender and the Media.* Cambridge, UK: Polity.

Gill, R. and Pratt, A., 2008. In the social factory? Immaterial labour, precariousness and cultural work. *Theory, culture & society, 25*(7–8), 1–30.

Goddard, M., & Parikka, J. (2011). Editorial: Unnatural ecologies. *Fibreculture Journal, 17.*

Gordon, J. (2007). The mobile phone and the public sphere: Mobile phone usage in three critical situations. *Convergence, 13,* 307–319.

Grosz, E. A. (1994). *Volatile bodies: Toward a corporeal feminism.* Bloomington-Indianapolis: Indiana University Press.

Guha, P. (2015). Hash tagging but not trending: The success and failure of the news media to engage with online feminist activism in India. *Feminist Media Studies, 15*(1), 155–157.

Haraway, D. (1988). Situated knowledges: The science question in feminism and the privilege of partial perspective. *Feminist Studies, 14,* 575–599.

Haraway, D. J. (1997). *ModestWitness@SecondMillennium. FemaleManMeets OncoMouse: Feminism and technoscience.* New York: Routledge.

Hardt, M., & Negri, A. (2000). *Empire.* Cambridge, MA: Harvard University Press.

Hardt, M. and Negri, A. (2005). *Multitude: War and democracy in the age of empire*. Penguin.

Horeck, T. (2014). #AskThicke:'Blurred lines', rape culture, and the feminist hashtag takeover. *Feminist Media Studies, 14*(6), 1105–1107.

Isin, E., & Ruppert, E. (2015). *Being digital citizens*. London: Rowman & Littlefield.

Jarrett, K. (2016). *Feminism, labour and digital media: The digital housewife*. London: Routledge.

Juris, J. S. (2005). The new digital media and activist networking within anti-corporate globalization movements. *The Annals of the American Academy of Political and Social Science, 597*, 189–208.

Kalajdzievski, S. (2008). *Math and art: An introduction to visual mathematics*. Boca Raton: CRC Press.

Kaun, A. (2015). 'This space belongs to us!': Protest spaces in times of accelerating capitalism. In L. Dencik & O. Leistert (Eds.), *Critical perspectives on social media and protest: Between control and emancipation*. London: Rowman & Littlefield.

Kember, S. (2003). *Cyberfeminism and artificial life*. London: Routledge.

Kember, S., & Zylinska, J. (2012). *Life after new media: Mediation as a vital process*. Cambridge, MA: MIT Press.

Kennedy, H. (2016). Why study social media data mining?. In *Post, mine, repeat*, 19–39. Palgrave Macmillan UK.

Laclau, E. (2001). Can immanence explain social struggles?. *Diacritics, 31*(4), 3–10.

Lash, S., & Lury, C. (2007). *Global culture industry: The mediation of things*. Cambridge: Polity.

Law, J., & Mol, A. (2002). *Complexities: Social studies of knowledge practices*. Durham: Duke University Press.

Lawrence, C., & Shapin, S. (1998). *Science incarnate: Historical embodiments of natural knowledge*. Chicago: University of Chicago Press.

Love, H. (2009). *Feeling backward*. Cambridge: Harvard University Press.

Loza, S. (2014). Hashtag feminism, # solidarityIsForWhiteWomen, and the other# femfuture. *Ada: A Journal of Gender, New Media, and Technology, 5, np*.

Martinot, S. (2001). *Maps and mirrors: Topologies of art and politics*. Evanston, IL: Northwestern University Press.

Massanari, A. (2015). # Gamergate and the happening: How Reddit's algorithm, governance, and culture support toxic technocultures. *New Media & Society* 1461444815608807.

Mattoni, A. (2012). *Media practices and protest politics: How precarious workers mobilise*. London: Routledge.

Mazzola, G., GöLler, S., & MüLler, S. (2002). *The topos of music: Geometric logic of concepts, theory, and performance*. Boston, MA: Birkhauser Verlag.

Mccall, L. (2005). The complexity of intersectionality. *Signs, 30,* 1771–1800.

Mcrobbie, A. (2007). Post feminism and popular culture: Bridget Jones and the new gender regime. In Y. Tasker & D. Negra (Eds.), *Interrogating postfeminism: Gender and the politics of popular culture* (pp. 27–39). Durham, NC: Duke University Press.

Milioni, D. L. (2009). Probing the online counterpublic sphere: The case of Indymedia Athens. *Culture and Society, 31,* 409–431.

Mohanty, C. T. (1988). Under Western eyes: Feminist scholarship and colonial discourses. *Feminist Review,* 61–88.

Mohanty, C. T. (2003). *Feminism without borders: Decolonizing theory, practicing solidarity.* London: Duke University Press.

Mouffe, C. (2005 [1993]). *The return of the political.* London: Verso.

Munt, S. (1998). *Queer attachments: The cultural politics of shame.* London: Ashgate.

Murphy, M. (2012). *Seizing the means of reproduction: Entanglements of feminism, health, and technoscience.* Durham, NC: Duke University Press.

Naimzada, A. K., Stefani, S., & Torriero, A. (2009). *Networks, topology and dynamics theory and applications to economics and social systems.* Berlin: Springer.

O'Riordan, K. (2010). *The genome incorporated: Constructing biodigital identity.* Farnham: Ashgate Publishing Ltd.

Papacharissi, Z. (2002). The virtual sphere: The internet as a public sphere. *New Media & Society, 4,* 9–27.

Plant, S. (1997). *Zeros + ones: Digital women and the new technoculture.* New York: Doubleday.

Postill, J. (2009). What is the point of media anthropology?. *Social Anthropology, 17*(3), 334–337.

Rentschler, C. (2015). # Safetytipsforladies: Feminist Twitter takedowns of victim blaming. *Feminist Media Studies, 15*(2), 353–356.

Rentschler, C. A. (2014). Rape culture and the feminist politics of social media. *Girlhood Studies, 7*(1), 65–82.

Ruiz, P. (2014). *Articulating dissent: Protest and the public sphere.* London: Pluto Press.

Shakhsari, S. (2011). Weblogistan goes to war: Representational practices, gendered soldiers and neoliberal entrepreneurship in diaspora. *Feminist Review, 99,* 6–24.

Silverstone, R. (2002). Complicity and collusion in the mediation of everyday life. *New Literary History, 33,* 761–780.

Stephansen, H. C. (2016). Understanding citizen media as practice: Agents, processes, publics. In M. Baker & B. Blaagaard (Eds.), *Citizen media and public spaces: Diverse expressions of citizenship and dissent.* London: Routledge,

Stephansen, H. C., & Couldry, N. (2014). Understanding micro-processes of community building and mutual learning on Twitter: A 'small data' approach. *Information, Communication & Society, 17*(10), 1212–1227.

Stone, A. R. (1995). *The war of desire and technology at the close of the mechanical age.* Cambridge, MA: MIT Press.

Terranova, T. (2004). *Network culture: Politics for the information age.* London: Pluto Press.

Thompson, C. (2005). *Making parents: The ontological choreography of reproductive technologies.* Cambridge, MA: MIT Press.

Touraine, A. (1981). *The voice and the eye: An analysis of social movements.* Cambridge: Cambridge University Press.

Turkle, S. (1996). *Life on the screen: Identity in the age of the Internet.* London: Weidenfeld & Nicolson.

Van Dijck, J. (2013). *The culture of connectivity.* Oxford: Oxford University Press.

Volkmer, I. (2014). *The global public sphere: Public communication in the age of reflective interdependence.* Cambridge: Polity.

Wakeford, N. (1997). Cyberqueer. In S. Munt & A. Medhurst (Eds.), *The lesbian and gay studies reader.* London: Cassell.R.

CHAPTER 2

Women's Organisations and the Social Imaginary of Networked Feminism: Digital and Networked by Default?

Digital networks are efficient when it comes to sharing information, but this is not their only function; online, actors come together in real time to 'make things public' (Latour and Weibel 2005), to frame public concerns in unique ways and to claim voice and recognition (Couldry 2010). Digital networks in the so-called Web 2.0 era are indeed becoming a space of civil society. But is feminism becoming networked, and are we moving into an era of 'digital sisterhood'? Although they have been some-times heralded as a primary site for activism, because of their intrinsic social and participatory aspects, I suggest in this chapter that Web 2.0 platforms still complement existing activist practices.

Indeed, network technologies today offer the possibility for high speed, far-reaching campaigning, and connecting across space and time. Meanwhile, mobile phone users who cannot afford a personal computer can now access the internet. But for an organisation to function just using mobile phones is not enough. As I argue here, setting up digital infra-structures within organisations results in prioritising processes of on-going change, training and innovation, at the expense of other, more sustained forms of engagement. This may be detrimental for those women's groups that are under-resourced due to public spending cuts. I do not mean to deny that digital infrastructure and training are crucial for feminist third-sector organisations. But I think that we should approach the complexity of digital media for activists through grounding our inquiry in the values

© The Author(s) 2016
A. Fotopoulou, *Feminist Activism and Digital Networks*,
Palgrave Studies in Communication for Social Change,
DOI 10.1057/978-1-137-50471-5_2

and practices of feminists, and in the situated conditions in which social actors operate, if we are to avoid recreating grand narratives of unified digital presence – and the exclusionary implications of such narratives.

But where does this widespread assumption that social networking and other media technologies are central for women's organisations stem from? We can trace this tendency to accommodate digital communications and technological innovation as an already proved and desirable solution for activist organisations in what has been framed as the 'cultural logic of computation' (Golumbia 2009) and elsewhere, 'the regime of computation' (Hayles 2005). In the second part of the chapter, I provide a substantive account of the discourses, values and ideologies that circulate and that join gender-related political activity to extensive use of digital media. These, I argue, contribute to a shared 'social imaginary' (Taylor 2004) of networked feminism and legitimate political engagement. As we will see, these to a large extent guide digital media practices. There are four sets of discourses: (1) dominant framings of digital engagement and digital inclusion, (2) dominant framings of the digital way of life as a productive and progressive 'good life', (3) cyberfeminism and (4) utopian cyber-libertarian narratives.

Drawing on ethnography with feminist organisations based in London, I will next investigate understandings of networked connectivity among participants, and also the hopes and fears that informed their organisational and individual decisions and media practices. The empirical material is collected through interviews with organisations and individuals who are members of a wide and diverse UK feminist network, inspired by the Women's Liberation Movement. As we will see, my research findings suggest that, for women's groups today, the desire to connect echoes the libertarian promises of Web 2.0 as an 'open' and 'shared' space. Participants recognised that processes of computerisation are widespread, and that some form of digital engagement was necessary: first, they have to compete with established structures of institutional power – for instance, by responding to governmental consultations, where agenda issues are already defined by powerful actors; second, they have to compete for political voice, recognition and publicity in online spaces where other social actors campaign. They were thus concerned about their role and their capacity as situated political subjects, when the default mode of campaigning and communication for activists seemed to have become digital and networked. Of course, feminist politics are a moving target and it is difficult to capture how they evolve whilst technologies are also changing. At the same time, there are differences between groups with a long history (such as the Fawcett Society[1]) and organisations that have emerged after Web 2.0, not only politically, but also in their understandings of technology. What is more, in the UK the language of feminist waves has less hold among feminists than in the USA, and it is the re-invigoration of the principles and histories of the Women's Liberation Movement that characterises contemporary British feminism. I acknowledge these differences (between generations of activists, technological literacies and political agendas); but I also find it important to identify commonalities among feminists in their motivations for new communicative practices, in order to more fully understand the relationship between networked media and activism for social change.

The context of this research is a climate of widespread economic crisis in the UK,[2] which led to funding cuts for most grassroots feminist groups,[3] including refuges for trafficked women, such as Eaves4Women (Townsend 2011), and Rape Crisis provisions across the capital (Rape Crisis 2009). During the period of my study, the final Parliamentary Readings of the Policing and Crime Bill 2009 (now an Act) were taking place. Therefore the issues prominent on the agendas of most activist groups at the time largely concurred with the reforms proposed in the Bill.[4] For example, the theme of the Feminism in London conference was: 'Pornification, the pay gap, eating disorders...Where do we go from here?', and it dealt with prostitution. At the same time, changes in the digital communications landscape, shaped to a large extent by the Digital Economy Act and Ofcom, are paving the way for public services (e.g. eLearning, eGovernment, eHealth) to become 'digital by default' (Helsper 2008). In this context of digital – and, I would like to add, *networked* – by default, feminist organisations find themselves rethinking their allocation of resources, in order to best accommodate the setting up of digital platforms and networks, and at the same time, to maintain their political and social aims of supporting women.

DIGITAL ENGAGEMENT, CYBERFEMINISM AND COMPUTATIONAL NARRATIVES

Digital engagement is often used to describe the adoption of a set of digital media practices (social media, email, websites) by both civil society organisations and individuals from marginalised groups that are also usually targeted by governmental agencies. Framed as 'any use of social media by a corporate organisation, right through to more specific definitions around how public sector organs promote participation in policymaking' (Helpful Technology 2013, n.p.), it often takes merely the form of consultations on existing governmental websites and platforms (see Government Digital Service 2016). Instead of digital engagement, governmental rhetoric shows preference for the term 'digital inclusion'. For instance, having identified that 150 million Europeans (30%) have never used the internet, the 2010 European-wide directive Digital Agenda for Europe has proposed interventions that relate mainly to web access for socially disadvantaged groups (age group 65–74, low income, unemployed, less educated, people with disabilities) and minors; and to overcoming barriers to this participation.[5] If we accept these narratives to be the dominant framings of a 'digital way of life' and a 'good life', we might want to question how such reiterations of liberal rhetoric – whereby the internet is seen as an opportunity for economic growth, both for the country and the individual (Mossberger et al. 2008) – are compatible with and conducive to activist aspirations for social justice and gender equality. Outside these framings, it is well established that online media increasingly form part of the communication of social movements and civil society politics (Atton 2002; Lovink 2002; Papacharissi 2002). Civic engagement and political participation, facilitated by the use of digital technologies, are today a democratic aspiration (Bruns 2008, Schäfer 2010). Feminists use networked media in order to stay connected and to engage new participants in their actions, and as Catherine Redfern and Kristin Aune (2010) recount in *Reclaiming the F-Word*, this means that new forms of feminism among younger women are emerging.

This dominant, liberal framing in EU and UK government discourse is complemented by a wider circulation of social imaginaries, which is specifically relevant to feminist actors. 'Social imaginaries' refer to the ways in which people imagine their social existence, social surroundings and their connections with others (Taylor 2004). They are carried in images, stories and legends, and are significant precisely because they 'make possible common practices and a widely shared sense of legitimacy' (Taylor 2004: 106). In the era of technoscientific globally networked societies, people imagine their social existence through both discursive and technical practices (Kelty 2005, 186), and it is through such practices, including the conditions of online access and web-linking behaviour, that feminist groups share a sense of legitimacy with other civil society actors.

Social and cultural imaginaries of technology and women have long been strong drives for visions and promises of a 'networked feminism'. Figurations of 'cyberfeminism', itself a contested notion and a self-reflexive movement, which have circulated since the 1990s (Paasonen 2011), play an important role in the performative articulation of this promise. As an art practice, the Australians VNS Matrix (1991) coined the term in 1991, claiming a feminine corporeality of technology with irony and subversion. Donna Haraway's (1991) cyborg metaphor, Sadie Plant's (1997) account of machines and women, and Allucquère Rosanne (Sandy) Stone's (1995) 'online fluidity', have all inspired how the internet has been imagined by feminist users during the last twenty years. These often techno-utopian visions of technology and women can be thought to occupy space alongside other more widespread imaginaries of the internet as an open space and Web 2.0 as a participatory, and hence distinctly empowering ecology for the individual user. US futurist technology 'gurus', intellectuals, entrepreneurs and media reportage have long-generated 'cyber-libertarian 2.0' discourses (Dahlberg 2010: 334) and Information and Communication Technologies (ICTs) and 'Web 2.0' models that operate widely in such imaginary modes (Bassett 2008). Google has built its whole marketing strategy on such a liberal imaginary of neutrality and not-for-profit publicness (Van Dijck 2013). The internet has been envisioned as a scarcity-fighting machine (Andrejevic 2013: 10) at a time when those who controlled information flow maintained political and social power. The ideological underpinnings of these imaginaries are necessary to analyse in relation to contemporary feminist activists, as activists are indeed driven by both visions of connectivity and by visions of a feminist movement. Such computational visions of social change, in other words visions of social change and sisterhood in which networked connectivity and ICTs are central, shape to a large extent the priorities of feminist activists. As the empirical analysis of this chapter suggests, these imaginaries are, at the same time, indications of a feminism with a distinct identity in networked environments, and symptoms of a prescribed and controlled mode of digital and networked engagement. At the same time, digital and networked practices become a key feature of these organs, their sense of who belongs in feminism as a social movement, and who is excluded from the identity 'feminist', which is often performed online.

In what follows, I present reflections that have emerged out of fieldwork with various women's organs, which are mainly volunteer-run and receive limited or no state funding. They occupy different positions in the political spectrum and have different campaign priorities: anti-pornography, anti-trafficking, poverty and equal pay, and rights of minority groups and asylum seekers. In this chapter, I draw on accounts recorded during in-depth semi-structured interviews with 12 activists, and during participant observation at various events organised by women's organs, including the Feminism in London 2009 Annual Conference, the Women's Resource Centre (WRC) 2010 Annual General Meeting and the 2010 'Women's Liberation Conference@40' at Ruskin College in Oxford. I interviewed participants in the Feminism in London Conference, an event of increasing centrality in British grassroots feminism, organised annually by the London Feminist Network (LFN) (a women-only feminist networking and campaigning organ established in 2004 that organises the annual Reclaim the Night event). Participating groups were Object, a human rights organ that challenges the sexual objectification of women through 'lads' mags', lap dancing clubs or sexist advertising; the Fawcett Society, a leading UK-charity campaigning about pensions, equal pay, poverty and social justice; the LFN; and the WRC, a national umbrella organ for women's charities, with over 500 members. I also interviewed journalist and Green Party candidate at the time Beatrix Campbell and psychoanalyst Susie Orbach. Some accounts have been anonymised, according to the wishes of research participants. This sample is by no means representative[6]; it captures, however, the heterogeneity of feminist actors and the different understandings of what feminist politics in digital networked environments mean today.

Versions of Contemporary Feminism and Network Imaginaries: Changing Organal Practices and Making Sense of Digital Media

'A building with women through its veins'

Most feminist activists who were interviewed for this chapter found Web 2.0 tools to be essential to their identity as active participants in a histori-cally long-standing feminist movement. Being active in online social net works in particular, by generating and circulating content, gave them a sense of connectedness with other feminists across space and time.[7]

Although for London women's groups there was clear orientation towards front-end practices of connectivity, these practices did not replace the offline habits that met their needs for connectedness and brought them together on an everyday basis, such as informal meetings and conferences. Nevertheless, participants to a large extent understood digital media and networks as technologies and spaces that enable intergenerational and 'translocal' (Hepp 2008) connections between feminists. This was of big value to them, and as a result, influenced their decisions about setting up new social media platforms, the degree to which they mobilised through them, and the form that this engagement took with and beyond social media.

One of the key actors in this network who prioritised the development of digital infrastructures was the WRC. The WRC perceived social media as a new space for activism and promoted the idea that online networking among women's organs is necessary for its affiliated members. It set up an online social networking platform called *The Café*, which in its two-month pilot phase involved 150 women's organs. A survey the WRC conducted about how women's organs use the internet found that 25% did not have their own website. The WRC understood this to indicate technophobia amongst women's organs. A sustained effort to overcome the scepticism among women's organs towards social media platforms was made by Sandra, the Centre's communications officer, who provided this training, including a printed step-by-step guide for using the *Café*.

Twitter had been significant for the WRC in many ways: it was used to locate funding opportunities, to learn about policy consultations, to recruit new members and to share relevant information with them. Sandra's enthusiasm for Twitter corresponds to a widespread perception of network media as transparent modes of communication. Echoing open architecture aspects of digital networks, alongside discourses of interactivity and participation, Sandra stressed that online communication media facilitate horizontal ways of connecting.[8] She used the metaphor of open architecture to explain how localised, individual and relatively small feminist organs can now connect in a common conversation, using a common language: 'It is a bit like opening the roof of an organ. People can dip in and out'.

Interestingly, at the Annual General Meeting of the WRC, the Chief Executive of the Centre used the building metaphor when she described their offline action plans. She envisioned a building in London that would host women's voluntary organs, 'a building with women through its veins'

(WRC AGM 2009). This latter vision of openness and collaboration then corresponds to a concrete version of the digital media open-roof organ. Although the building was physically placed in the centre of London, whereas the *Café* was virtually anywhere, both maintained the WRC as the central node of their connection. Keeping the WRC as the central node was essential, because the WRC maintained links to funding sources and to policymakers, which individual local charities often lacked. In this sense, the online platform not only brought charities in contact with one another, but additionally gave them a communication venue through which their concerns could reach officials.

The wider rhetoric of digital networks as sites of non-hierarchical modes of connection (Terranova 2004) and as elementary components of democratic participation underpinned the narrations of all participants. Networked feminism in this vision was a decentralised structure, which allowed women's groups to connect in an optimum way; *it is* ubiquitous and inclusive. Being part of 'the network' for many interviewees implied belonging in a wider movement that did not adhere to the limitations of 'waves'. For example, when Finn Mackay (2009), the spokesperson of the LFN, in our exchange described the action of the LFN and feminism more broadly in an email interview, she thought of it as a continuation of the Women's Liberation Movement. However, the LFN's vision of a unified political movement in an open digital space often came into direct conflict with the exclusionary practices that these feminists performed offline, on the ground: the LFN excluded trans women from its spaces, and in some cases, Reclaim the Night marches reinforced the exclusion of sex workers from feminism. At the same time, rather than perceiving their position in a feminist network as a local or micro-struggle in a horizontal assemblage, as for instance a 'multitude' (Hardt and Negri 2005) reading would have it, participants imagined the centre to be a physical place, London. Such exclusions (of marginalised groups and localities) are indicative of how social imaginaries of networked media as the facilitators of a unified feminist identity are often problematic when it is at odds with the material reality of which feminisms are permitted and demonstrated.

Catching Up with Technologies and Changing Organal Routines

Whilst the imaginary of instant high-speed transnational communication among feminists stimulated digital engagement for many of the groups, there was also a lot of anxiety about catching up with technologies.

Participants talked about their sense of a knowledge gap, a digital literacy gap, which was widening. Ellen Helsper (2008: 2) has argued that a 'digital underclass' is forming in Britain, and that 'as the government plans to make public services "digital by default" these individuals will be unable to access them, not because of a lack of infrastructure but because of a lack of (effective) take up of the available connections'. Indeed, older feminist activists who were part of the Women's Liberation Movement were particularly worried about isolation due to lack of connectivity, especially since they already felt that a generational gap distanced them from current developments and younger activists. For example, Beatrix Campbell (2009), responding as an individual, rather than as part of an organ, explained how for her new media literacy was a requirement for meeting the demands of digital audiences, and particularly of those who follow her journalistic and political activity:

> I know that that's generational, and I know that that's not useful...so it's kind of ambivalent, slightly technophobic, slightly utilitarian approach to new means of communication....Regularly, I realise I can't intervene, I didn't know my way around the kind of debates...so I do my thing and that's it....I have to become technically literate...I'm just going to change.

Media training seemed for many activists to be a key condition for acquiring representational space online. Participants used a language that expressed urgency, necessity – not merely opportunity.

> I feel we're not doing as well online, we need to catch up,...I'd like it to be the same amount of interaction as a workshop or an event, I'd like it to be just like that. (Morden 2009)

Although most groups and activists see the necessity of having a web presence, some understand their role as activists in stimulating dialogue and mobilisation to be more important than expressing the interests of a specific group. This diversity of such understandings is important because, as noted next, feminist engagement and communicative activity in digital networks is not just a matter of transmitting information, or exercising rational exchange in a new space; it also relates to a fear of being left out and of being forgotten. In the next section, I discuss the implications of media literacy and access to Web 2.0 digital culture for older feminists and their sense of being excluded and historically erased.

'That's our own Facebook, *we meet face-to-face': New Media Literacy and Offline Networking*

Seeking to address new media literacy, the South London Fawcett Group (SLFG) and others invested time and effort in making digital media part of their organ. Clearly, for those who worked at the WRC (younger and already familiar with Web 2.0 technologies) joining the new *Café* platform demanded little extra effort; they already had an everyday pattern of use of mobile media technologies and were tweeting from the Feminism in London 2009 conference (from here on FiL09). However, for older women of the SLFG, becoming members of a new platform took considerable effort; they already struggled to incorporate email technology in their organal mode of operation. The fact that as affiliated members, the SLFG received training from the Women's Resource Centre did not make much difference.

Implementing a social online networking platform, for example the Café or even Facebook, required as much work as domesticating Web 1.0 tools (email technology and email lists) for the SLFG. This is important because it shows that older women who lack digital skills and basic access cannot differentiate between Web 1.0 and Web 2.0, and therefore cannot benefit from the additional layers of connectivity, and subsequently political engagement, that are possible. As the following quote, from my interview with the spokesperson of the SLFG on 30 October 2009, shows, the channels of internal communication remain more or less the same:

> We have talked about having Facebook group, we don't have a Facebook group . . . but again to the older members it's a novelty, which we have to get accustomed to. In a way, we meet once per month, we have good discussions, that is sufficient. That's our own Facebook, we meet face-to-face.

This understanding is very different to the vision expressed by the WRC; what the WRC described as 'dipping in and out of organs', with the use of social media, seemed highly complicated and even utopian considering the reality of digital engagement for older women. Nonetheless, the SLFG had a fascinating story to narrate about the parallel evolution of their group and its digital capacity:

[The SLFG] has developed with the evolution of digital communications.... It happened so fast... And it is, quite a difference of experience
between older members and younger members... But on the whole *we try
to keep up, we can't, we can't, if we didn't people would not be interested in us.*
(SLFG 2009) (my emphasis)

In this narration, digital engagement and new networking communication
technologies are not exciting opportunities – they are *a one-way street*.
Participants felt they *ought* to be producing digital texts, or else the world
will pass them by. Combined with the narration of the ease with which
younger activists adopt social media and digital technologies more generally, a key concern is expressed here: primarily, there is a fear of exclusion
from political life and social life more generally, of older feminists and their
histories. The implications of this concern are important because they
challenge the assumed legitimacy of new communication technologies
when they become the measure for political engagement.

DIGITAL SISTERHOOD?

Material Constrains and the Struggle for Legitimacy

As it emerges from this fieldwork, the changing attitudes to and
practices of political engagement for various activist groups are influenced by a dynamic set of feelings and experiences: enthusiasm, uncertainty and fear. The enthusiasm about participation, openness and
connectivity ensues from the dominant understandings of connectivity
that circulate today and which constitute, following notions of social
imaginary (Kelty, Mansell, Taylor, Van Dijck), the 'network imaginary'
for feminists today. Enthusiasm about the potential of creative and
shared production for feminist activism is complemented by uncertainty about the conditions of heterogeneity and decentral. David
Morley (2001) and Arjun Appadurai (1996) have early on talked
about the destabilising effects of global and about how the sense of
place and neighbourhood shifts with network communications. Here,
the distinct sense of finding one's place and belonging in feminism and
digital environments is historically reworked in the notion of 'sisterhood': although criticised (Hooks 1986), the notion of 'sisterhood' –
initially suggested by Robin Morgan (1970) – can still be thought to
accommodate what *Deborah Rosenfelt and Judith Stacey wrote is the*

need to 'develop cultural forms that fill some of the...longings for intimacy, interdependency, and emotional security' (1987: 46) *for feminists. Digital networks contribute to the building of such cultural forms, of what could be termed as 'digital sisterhood', where feminist groups and women turn for support. However, as has been noted, this sisterhood as neighbourhood is located at the intersections of online spaces with the everyday offline physical interactions.*

The tension between insecurity and intention to participate in digital networks for the development of a 'digital sisterhood' is of course experienced by feminist activists today not as individuals, but as collectivities who claim a legitimate political voice, in a fast-paced technologically advanced world. Today, and after the Arab Spring revolutions, it appears as if ephemeral media and digital connections value more than the long, lived histories of political movements (Curran et al. 2011). In such a context of immediacy and ephemerality, the challenge for feminist activists is to validate the temporalities of slow, offline tactics, and long and often tiresome processes of campaigning, or the hectic activities when protesting on the street.

This struggle for meaning and legitimacy is ever so important for these feminist groups because they have to compete for voice (Couldry 2010) in the public sphere from a position of limited or absent funding, and as is evidenced above, low digital literacy. One example of limited resources is that the organ *Anybody* did not have a volunteer role exclusively for website moderation, which in turn affected the amount of interaction with the people using the website. Susie Orbach, speaking to me as the organ's spokesperson, stressed: 'It's all informal and voluntary. So you might get a twenty-year-old, who comes and says she's going to set a zine up, she's going to do this, but then it doesn't deliver necessarily' (2009).

While maintaining a multiple web presence was challenging for organs that did not change their mode of operation on a wider scale, for the LFN the email list was their constitutive activity. It was created through two previous and now discontinued online mailing lists, the *UK Feminist Action* and the *London 3rd Wave*. With approximately 600 members on their list at the time of the study, the LFN mainly focused on disseminating information from the Women in London calendar of events. Thus although many groups did not have a communicative strategy guiding how, when or why they would adopt digital networking, they strived to get connected, because they understood this as a key aspect of maintaining activist engagement.

Meanwhile, *Object!* 'a human rights organ which challenges the sexual objectification of women in the media and popular culture' (*Object!* 2009), demonstrated a succinct communicative strategy. This media strategy was indicative of their role as mediators between grassroots activists and the government: the website in the case of *Object!* was primarily a collection of resources, such as template letters to send to members of parliament (MPs). *Object!* additionally maintained a Yahoo! Group and a blog, which targeted activists. Part of their activist support was to supply evidence for community groups to use in court hearings or in council targeted motions against lap-dancing clubs opening in their area. Apart from acting as mediators between the government and activists, *Object!* as an organ aimed at attracting mainstream media attention to their campaigns. Having the mainstream media report on these campaigns is arguably an important means of reaching out to wider audiences, and potentially brings debates to the public sphere. However, *Object!* did not entirely rely on social networks and provocative media campaigning to get their message across. Their communicative and organal activity was rather complex, and indeed one could even say dispersed and networked. It lends activist support to Eaves and Fawcett, who are organs with similar social power; it participates in a knowledge exchange and coordinates grassroots feminist groups who are starting up from zero-level activity. It aimed to 'share skills and build unity within the women's movement' (*Object!* 2009); and third, the organ functions as a communicative channel between feminist groups and mainstream media, for the expression of common concerns. Therefore, if we were to name *networked feminism* as a form of contemporary political action that is characterised by complex connectivity and which operates at the intersections of online and offline, and across campaigning activities, feelings and people, *Object!* would be exemplary.

My point here is that the intersection between online and offline is significant because it helps us question the bias towards online and always-connected forms of activism. This is a cultural bias that puts weight on social media or otherwise visible-on-the-screen networks, and is a symptom of a wider 'culture of connectivity' (Van Dijck 2013) in contemporary informational societies. In the next section, I elaborate this point by questioning the notion of 'networked feminism' as well as its currency in contemporary feminism, and by noting the tensions between the reality of new forms of exclusion and the promissory narratives of Web 2.0 participation.

Questioning Networked by Default: Social Imaginary,
Ideology and Digital Culture

Digital platforms, architectures, economies, in other words digital infrastructures, are becoming the default context where not only politics, but also life in
general takes place. Of course, the potential of internet technologies to
liberate the world has been seriously disputed in media studies, and the
widespread belief that they can has even been called a 'net delusion' in
relation to social media and the Arab Spring (Morozov 2011). Women's
groups in this study have certainly not been delusional about the internet's
potential for gender equality; however, my exploration evidenced that activists' attitudes were shaped by certain social imaginaries of networked politics,
participatory action and connectivity. These attitudes ranged from celebratory adoption of digital communication to resistance to social media platforms. Some groups set up websites and email lists; some were passionate
about Twitter; and others introduced social networking platforms and prioritised new media training. Despite the differences in the micro-practices of
organising and communicating between feminist participants, they shared
values and languages of network participation, and the promise of networked
feminism, but also the fear of being left behind and being left out.

The feminist groups and activists that I interviewed for this study were
not obsessed with updating their profiles and online visibility.
Nonetheless, some form of digital engagement seemed to be understood
as the condition for having political voice in the dissonance of neoliberal
politics, which reminds us 'why voice matters' (Couldry 2010). The
adoption of new communication technologies and social networking
within civic organs was also an indicator of progress and the ability to
'keep up'. This understanding of participation and empowerment is
problematically fused with productivity, administrative control and functionality, which are themselves ideological tools. There is a delicate
difference however, between the social imaginary of networked feminism
as a productive desire to keep up with technologies, and the understanding of digital engagement as the necessary and default condition for
legitimate political voice. This difference needs to be noted in relation
to current framings of interactivity, democracy and even activism as
fantasies of 'communicative capitalism' (Dean 2009), where social actors
are swayed by the desire to produce digital content. Jodi Dean suggests
that contemporary communicative environments are shaped by technological fetishism, which manifests in neoliberal fantasies of active and

participatory citizenship (Dean 2009). Although it is politically important to recognise, and continually reiterate, that neoliberalism is a global system that suffocates equality, thus far my examination of feminist groups' imaginaries relates less to abundance of mobile and web content. I agree that the circulation of computational discourses and internet imaginaries normalises computational (Golumbia 2009), reinforces wider power relations and reproduce dominant ideologies (Mansell 2012). Indeed, it is unclear how demands for recognition, such as gender and sexuality, which drive social struggles (Fraser and Honneth 2003), fit with framings of distributed power and democratic participation in Web 2.0, or how dominant framings of digital inclusion respond to activist aims. Here however, it is not my concern to draw a bleak picture of how computationalism and network technology failed to materialise the promise to deliver radical change in the global social and political fabric. Media studies is prolific in its ideological critique of computation (Berry 2011; Chun 2011; Fuchs 2011). I would rather like to argue that the social imaginary of digital and networked participation, which is complemented by the computational logic, has a dark side: exclusion from what appears as the era of unhindered citizen participation. In particular, women's groups in this study, like other contemporary civil society actors, participate in the online public sphere (Downing 2001; Gordon 2007) to different degrees; age, lack of resources and media literacy being the three most important factors that modulate this participation, and in some cases become new types of exclusions of access to publicity and recognition. Being neither hackers nor artists, these activists could not really work 'through protocol' (Galloway 2004) to achieve recognition. They lacked the necessary skills and resources that would allow them to resist the ubiquity of protocol. I noted how although Beatrix Campbell was initially sceptical, she eventually espoused Twitter and blogging as means for providing audiences with more choice and easier access to content. The SLFG, who were mostly older women, met face-to-face and humorously commented that this was *their* Facebook – but at the same time feared that they were 'no longer interesting to the world', as they put it. Although the issues relating to new forms of exclusion and the impact of internet technologies on everyday life have been analysed in earlier work (Miller and Slater 2000), Web 2.0 creates a distinct media environment for connectivity, because of its always-on and social networking characteristics. Therefore, the exclusions created are not plainly a matter of access and being online or offline, as was the case in the beginning of the 2000s; exclusions are more sophisticated and concern the frequency of updating online presence and producing more interesting content in social media.

To reiterate, the notion of 'default' in relation to digital and networked technologies is ideological because it refers not to how feminists *could* be producing an abundance of communicational texts and online content (social online platforms, newsletters or creative code), but that they *ought* to be producing them, or else the world will pass them by. The tension between *ought to* and *could* participate and be empowered can be thought as symptomatic of the promises of 'good life' and the 'digital way of life'. Sara Ahmed (2010) writes about the promise of good life, happiness and the good intentions behind it. The performative aspects of the promise order a future and make this future predictable, something to aim for. This promise and social imaginary of networked feminism, the online performance of a feminist identity, is a set of practices and discourses which shape social and cultural expectations about how life with digital media should be: digital media require our participation, our willingness to provide data for advertisers or for our own benefit. Participation and interactivity are becoming standard framings and the production of networked connections is central in the promise of empowerment. What makes the digital potentially political is the determination of people to connect, and to embody, in their communication practices, new forms of solidarity. The ethnographic study showed that women's groups were indeed positioned within this performative promise, while the underlying assumption seemed to be that they ought to become digital and networked by default.

The default aspect of interactive technologies signals the 'participatory web 2.0 as ideology' (Fuchs 2011: 257), and raises questions about the agency of social actors to position themselves in relation to it, and to shape their lives and political identity. The sense that activists ought to participate, and that networks are nowadays *the norm*, constitutes digital networks as a ubiquitous system and creates space for negotiation and opposition. Indeed, activists exercised their agency and often resisted the interactivity, open-sharing practices and reconfiguration that the model of 'digital and networked by default' represents. So far, when thinking about resistance in digital culture scholars have focused on forms of multi-actor ambivalence or resistance that relate to surveillance, face recognition and data harvesting, such as the United Kingdom National Identity Scheme (Martin et al. 2009). Other expressions of resistance to new media, which mainly respond to the assumed negative impact of digital technologies on the quality of family life and the development of youth, is by civic groups such as Slow Media (for digital disenchantment) or the National Day of Unplugging (http://nationaldayofunplugging.com/). If we think of everyday life and digital engagement as a form of free labour (Terranova 2013), non-consumption automatically constitutes actors as non-producers (Portwood-Stacer 2012). As Laura Portwood-Stacer argues, refusing to participate in social media, quitting Facebook or never joining it in the first place can form a part in resistance struggles, but it can also be a site for the representation of those struggles over meaning and resistance. Although, in the case of older feminists of the SLFG, the refusal articulated by 'this is our Facebook' is not necessarily an act of everyday resistance of the magnitude of a consumer strike (Cohen 2003; De Certeau 1984), it exemplifies how activists define the penetration of physical social spaces by online media. By becoming what Ahmed (2010) would call 'unwilling subjects', these London feminists resisted, or negotiated, not only their digital identity but also their political identity and their place in what appears to be a dominant digital culture which regulates how activists should connect nowadays. When they say 'we meet face to face, this is our Facebook', the women of SFWG acknowledge that Facebook is the dominant form of connecting and additionally marks the new space for doing politics. This acknowledgement but unwillingness to participate (to be part, to be regulated) reinstates that feminist politics, although in dialogue with the digital, are not subsumed in the digital. As the previous discussion about the cultural forms of a 'digital sisterhood' has shown, contemporary activists produce their own spaces and conditions for doing politics, even as the dominant culture of computationalism and networked by default seems to offer one universal set of practices for all political subjects. The agency of social actors who, in their own right, delineate how social media can be useful for their political aims, and how the 'digital and networked by default' is something to be afraid of, or opposed to, cannot be questioned. We may, however, want to problematise what it means for social agency more generally when political actors are legitimate only when operating with reference to a default context and their sole means of resistance are to 'opt-out'.

CONCLUSION: FEMINISM IS THE POLITICS
OF CONNECTIVITY AND AFFECT

Reading digital networks solely as public sphere (Downing 2001), as spaces of activist opportunity (Galloway 2004), spaces of web content abundance (Dean 2009) or 'digital enclosure' (Andrejevic 2007) limits how feminist politics can be understood. In this chapter, I have taken a step towards a fuller understanding of the communicative practices among a diverse group of London-based women's organs: I have accounted for the imaginaries of computational ubiquity and user empowerment in Web 2.0; the fears of being historically and politically erased; and their everyday negotiations and resistances. These three aspects paint a more complex picture of what digital media mean for feminist activists today, beyond the often uncritical celebration of Twitter and other social networking platforms. My analysis offers clear indications that, in the shared space of increased visibility and connectivity, feminists experience new forms of exclusion from access to publicity and recognition, as digital networks can be, at the same time, spaces of uncertainty and empowerment, depending on skills, resources and age. But access is not the only form of exclusion. Today, the neoliberal myth of more choice is paired with the myth of producing more content in digital networks. The exclusions of today's digital networks are more sophisticated than ten years ago. The frequency of updating online presence and producing more interesting content in social media, in other words the struggle for visibility through intense productivity and user unpaid labour, are central here. Feminist organs that simply cannot afford a communications officer, who will be solely responsible for tweeting or populating Facebook pages, are automatically excluded from a post-feminist networked space of Twitter feminist wars over representation, selfie feminism or from a wider map of slacktivism (see Chapter 3 for a more detailed discussion on this). In effect, the complexity of social relationships and the slow temporal character of political processes, which are so essential in the practices of activist groups, are suffocated with digital technologies.

The social imaginary of 'networked feminism' as an ideological construct of legitimate political engagement in the 'open' and 'shared' space of Web 2.0 technologies is cultivated by widely circulating narratives, including those of digital inclusion, and encouraged by the reality of public services becoming digital by default in the UK. However, the fact that ageing and media literacy were sticking points in the ways in which activists perceived themselves as political subjects in highly mediated environments opens up wider questions about the viability, or even necessity, of a feminism which is digital and networked by default. Historically feminist politics have been a politics of connectivity and affect; they have developed through networks, connections and relationships, which have produced knowledge and lived experiences (Jolly and Roseneil 2012). We should thus keep rethinking the possibilities offered for social change by the changing environment of digital communications, but it is important to do so by looking at how the promises and imaginaries of a 'networked feminism' and 'digital sisterhood' translate into communicative practices of women's organs, as they are situated within material conditions of limited funding and shaped by embodied experiences of ageing.

Notes

1. The Fawcett Society was established in 1866.
2. In 2010, after £6.2 billion in budget cuts over half of women's organs have lost funding, year on year, since 2009; up to 40.6% in local authority spending on violence against women and girls' services (north East Women's Network 2013). In 2016, analysis by the House of Commons library shows that 86% of savings from tax and benefit changes since 2010, including those in the 2016 Budget, will have come from women. This is up from 81% after the joint Autumn Financial Statement and Comprehensive Spending Review in November 2015. Analysis undertaken by the Women's Budget Group demonstrates that by 2020, ten years of austerity measures will have had a regressive, gender-biased impact on household disposable income and living standards. The lowest income households and women will be hardest hit, with female lone parents and female single pensioners, seeing an average annual drop in living standards drop of 20% by 2020 (Women's Budget Group 2016)
3. Although feminist debates about misogyny, racism and feminism are an everyday occurrence in Twitter and the feminist blogosphere, here my focus is less with individuals, and more on the motivations and implications of networked connectivity for community and volunteer sector organs, with a wider gender equality agenda. See also fandom in relation to political, activism and Web 2.0 (Jenkins and Shresthova 2012).
4. These were namely the regulation of lap dancing clubs, creating Brothel Closure Orders and creating a new criminal offence of paying for sexual services of a prostitute controlled for gain (Home Office 2009: 37).

5. The Commission has identified seven obstacles to what is understood as 'a digital way of life' for European citizens (European Commission 2010: 5). These are: Fragmented digital markets, Lack of interoperability, Rising cybercrime and risk of low trust in networks, Lack of investment in networks, Insufficient research and innovation efforts, Lack of digital literacy and skills, Missed opportunities in addressing societal challenges.
6. It is estimated that there are currently 1273 women's organs in the UK (WRC 2011).
7. It might be useful here to distinguish between connectivity and connectedness. As Jose Van Dijck (2013) explains, there is a wider shift in the behaviours of internet users, from practices of connectedness to practices of connectivity; van Dijck focuses on the information that social media corporations use profitably, at the expense of, by harvesting invisible back-end data.
8. Open architecture is the design principle of the internet, introduced by Robert Hahn and Vincent Cerf at DARPA, which denotes that individual and autonomous networks connect to the internet through common bridging protocols (e.g. TCP/IP, URL, FTP, IRC) (Chadwick 2006).

BIBLIOGRAPHY

Ahmed, S. (2010). *The promise of happiness*. Durham, NC: Duke University Press.
Andrejevic, M. (2007). Surveillance in the digital enclosure. *The Communication Review, 10*(4), 295–317.
Andrejevic, M. (2013). *Infoglut: How too much information is changing the way we think and feel*. London: Routledge.
Appadurai, A. (1996). *Modernity at large: Cultural dimensions of globalization*. Minneapolis: University of Minnesota Press.
Atton, C. (2002). *Alternative media*. London: Sage.
Bassett, C. (2008). New maps for old?: The cultural stakes of '2.0'. *Fibreculture Journal, 13*.
Bennett, K. (2009). No trafficking? Well, there's a hell of a lot of women suffering. *The Observer* 25 October. http://www.guardian.co.uk/commentisfree/2009/oct/25/catherine-bennett-prostitution-trafficking. Accessed 17 July 2012.
Berry, D. (2011). *The philosophy of software*. London: Palgrave Macmillan.
Braidotti, R. (1996). Cyberfeminism with a difference. http://www.let.uu.nl/womens_studies/rosi/cyberfem.htm.
Bruns, A. (2008). *Blogs, Wikipedia, second life, and beyond: From production to produsage*. New York: Peter Lang.
Campbell, B. (2009). No Title. Interviewed by Aristea Fotopoulou. [MP3 Audio recording]. London: British Library, 21 November 2009.

Chadwick, A. (2006). *Internet politics: States, citizens, and new communication technologies*. Oxford: Oxford University Press.

Chun, W. H. K. (2011). *Programmed visions: Software and memory*. Cambridge, MA: The MIT Press.

Cohen, L. (2003). *A consumers' republic: The politics of mass consumption in Postwar America*. New York: Vintage.

Couldry, N. (2010). *Why voice matters: Culture and politics after neoliberalism*. London: Sage Publications.

Curran, J., Fenton, N., & Freedman, D. (2012). *Misunderstanding the internet*. London: Routledge.

Dahlberg, L. (2010). Cyber-libertarianism 2.0: A discourse theory/critical political economy examination. *Cultural Politics: An International Journal, 6,* 331–356.

De Certeau, M. (1984). *The practice of everyday life*. Berkeley: University of California Press.

Dean, J. (2009). *Democracy and other neoliberal fantasies: Communicative capitalism and left politics*. Durham, NC: Duke University Press.

Downing, J. (2001). *Radical media: Rebellious communication and social movements*. California: Sage Publications.

European Commission. (2010) Digital agenda for Europe. http://europa.eu/pol/pdf/flipbook/en/digital_agenda_en.pdf. Accessed 10 August 2013.

Fraser, N., & Honneth, A. (2003). *Redistribution or recognition? A political-philosophical exchange*. London: Verso.

Fuchs, C. (2011). *Foundations of critical media and information studies*. New York: Routledge.

Galloway, A. R. (2004). *Protocol: How control exists after decentralization*. Cambridge, MA: MIT Press.

Gates, K. (2011). *Our biometric future: Facial recognition technology and the culture of surveillance*. New York: NYU Press.

Golumbia, D. (2009). *The cultural logic of computation*. Cambridge, MA: Harvard University Press.

Gordon, J. (2007). The mobile phone and the public sphere: Mobile phone usage in three critical situations. *Convergence, 13*(3), 307–319.

Government Digital Service (2016) Blog: Government digital service. https://gds.blog.gov.uk. Accessed 10 July 2016.

Haraway, D. J. (1991). *Simians, cyborgs, and women: The reinvention of nature*. London: Free Association Books.

Hardt, M., & Negri, A. (2005). *Multitude: War and democracy in the age of empire*. New York: Penguin.

Hayles, N. K. (2005). *My mother was a computer: Digital subjects and literary texts*. Chicago: University of Chicago Press.

Helpful Technology. (2013). The digital engagement guide. www.digitalengagement.info.

Helsper, E. J. (2008). *Digital inclusion an analysis of social disadvantage and the information society.* London: Department for Communities and Local Government. http://www.communities.gov.uk/documents/communities/pdf/digitalinclusionanalysis.

Hepp, A. (2008). *Connectivity, networks and flows: Conceptualising contemporary communications.* Cresskill, NJ: Hampton Press.

Home Office (2009). Violence against women and girls strategy. *Home Office.* http://www.homeoffice.gov.uk/crime/violence-against-women-girls/. Accessed 25 November 2009.

Hooks, B. (1986). Sisterhood: Political solidarity between women. *Feminist Review, 23,* 125–138.

Object! (2009). *Anna van Heeswijk.* Interview at the Feminism in London 2009 Conference as the Grassroots Coordinator of Object. Interviewed by Aristea Fotopoulou. [MP3 Audio recording]. London: Conway Hall. 10 October 2009.

Jenkins, H., & Shresthova, S. (2012). Up, up, and away! The power and potential of fan activism. *Transformative Works and Cultures, 10.* http://testjournal.transformativeworks.org/index.php/twc/article/view/435/305.

Jolly, M., & Roseneil, S. (2012). Researching women's movements: An introduction to FEMCIT and sisterhood and after. *Women's Studies International Forum, 35*(3), 125–128. ISSN 0277-5395.

Kelty, C. (2005). Geeks, social imaginaries, and recursive publics. *Cultural Anthropology, 20*(2), 185–214.

Latour, B., & Weibel, P. (2005). *Making things public: Atmospheres of democracy.* Cambridge, MA: MIT Press.

Lovink, G. (2002). *Dark fiber: Tracking critical internet culture.* Cambridge, MA: MIT Press.

Mackay, F. (2009). No Title. Interviewed by Aristea Fotopoulou [Email questionnaire] Brighton. 22 November 2009.

Mansell, R. (2012). *Imagining the internet: Communication, innovation, and governance.* Oxford: Oxford University Press.

Martin, A. K., Van Brakel, A., & Bernhard, D. (2009). Understanding resistance to digital surveillance: Towards a multi-disciplinary, multi-actor framework. *Surveillance & Society, 6*(3), 213–232.

Matrix, V. N. S. (1991). Cyberfeminist manifesto for the 21st century. http://www.obn.org/reading_room/manifestos/html/cyberfeminist.html.

Miller, D., & Slater, D. (2000). *The internet: An ethnographic approach.* Oxford: Berg Publishers.

Morden, R. (2009). Interview with the artistic director of Scary Little Girls. Interviewed by Aristea Fotopoulou. [MP3 Audio recording]. London: Conway Hall. 10 October 2009.

Morgan, R. (1970). *Sisterhood is powerful.* New York: Vintage Books.

Morley, D. (2001). Belongings: Place, space and identity in a mediated world. *European Journal of Cultural Studies, 4*(4), 425–448.

Morozov, E. (2011). *The net delusion: How not to liberate the world.* London: Penguin.

Mossberger, K., Tolbert, C. J., & McNeal, R. S. (2008). *Excerpts from digital citizenship: The internet, society, and participation.* Cambridge, MA.: MIT Press, 2007. *First Monday, 13*, 2.

North East Women's Network. (2013). *The health of the women's sector in the North East of England.* http://www.newwomens.net/newwp-contentup loads/The_case_for_womens_services_14_11_13_2.pdf

Orbach, S. (2009). *Interview at the feminism in London 2009 conference.* Interviewed by Aristea Fotopoulou. [MP3 Audio recording]. London: Conway Hall. 10 October 2009.

Paasonen, S. (2011). Revisiting cyberfeminism. *Communications, 36*, 335–352.

Papacharissi, Z. (2002). The virtual sphere: The internet as a public sphere. *New Media & Society, 4*(1), 9–27.

Plant, S. (1997). *Zeros + ones: Digital women and the new technoculture.* London: Fourth Estate.

Portwood-Stacer, L. (2012). Anti-consumption as tactical resistance: Anarchists, subculture, and activist strategy. *Journal of Consumer Culture, 12*(1), 87–105.

Rape Crisis. (2009). North London Fawcett Group [blog]. https://nlfg.word press.com/rape-crisis-campaign/. Accessed 25 April 2011.

Rebecca Morden. (2009). Interview with the artistic director of Scary Little Girls. Interviewed by Aristea Fotopoulou. [MP3 Audio recording] Conway Hall, London, 10 October 2009.

Redfern, C., & Aune, K. (2010). *Reclaiming the F word: The new feminist movement.* London: Zed.

Rosenfelt, D., & Stacey, J. (1987). Second thoughts on the second wave. *Feminist Studies, 13*(2), 41–61.

Schäfer, M. (2010). *Bastard culture! User participation and the extension of cultural industries.* Amsterdam: Amsterdam University Press.

South London Fawcett Group. (SLFG). (2009). Interview with the spokesperson. Interviewed by Aristea Fotopoulou. [MP3 Audio recording]. Home location, London, 30 October 2009.

Stone, A. R. (1995). *The war of desire and technology at the close of the mechanical age.* Cambridge, MA: MIT Press.

Taylor, C. (2004). *Modern social imaginaries.* Durham: Duke University Press.

Terranova, T. (2004). *Network culture: Politics for the information age.* London: Pluto Press.

Terranova, T. (2012). Free labour. In T. Scholz (Ed.), *Digital labor: The internet as playground and factory* (pp. 33–57). London: Routledge.

Terranova, T. (2013). Debt and Autonomy: Lazzarato and the Constituent Powers of the Social. The New Reader: 1. http://thenewreader.org/Issues/1/DebtAndAutonomy. Accessed 2 December 2016

Townsend, M. (2011). Sex-trafficked women's charity Poppy project in danger as funding withdrawn, *The Observer* 17 April. http://www.guardian.co.uk/society/2011/apr/17/prostitution-human-trafficking. Accessed 17 July 2012.

Van Dijck, J. (2013). *The culture of connectivity*. Oxford: Oxford University Press.

Women's Budget Group. (2016). The impact on women of the 2016 budget: Women paying for the chancellor's tax cuts. http://wbg.org.uk/wp-content/uploads/2016/03/WBG_2016Budget_FINAL_Apr16.pdf

WRC. (2009). Women's Resource Centre Annual General Meeting. [MP3 Audio recording]. London, 19 November 2009.

WRC. (2011). Assessing the financial vulnerability of charities serving women. http://www.wrc.org.uk/includes/documents/cm_docs/2011/a/assessing_the_financial_vulnerabality_of_charities_serving_women.pdf

The Paradox of Feminism, Technology and Pornography: Value and Biopolitics in Digital Culture

If the premise of this book is that feminist and queer activist identities are being reconfigured with digital media, how do bodies with sexuality, passion and emotions relate, act and work with digital media technologies? The internet, the mobile devices and apps that are habitually used to connect are neither cold and wired, as was imagined in cyberpunk novels, in their early days, nor ethereal and wireless. In line with the approaches of cyberfeminists and artists who envision the flow of bits and bodily fluids through the network, I too think of the digital as world-within-the-'real' world, where bodies labour, sweat and sigh. As users generate endlessly more content in social media platforms, such as selfies, and information becomes abundant to an unprecedented magnitude, these live and fleshy bodies become ever so visible, not only in what has been traditionally considered porn, but also in the genres that are marginally pornographic. Selfie culture, and the ensuing 'selfie feminism' or fourth-wave feminism, are developments that have gained a lot of academic and media attention in the last few years. Self-exposure and surveillance in digital culture have a double edge – both empowering for female users, and at the same time, risky and potentially harmful.

A fundamental concern with sexual politics and pornography is the central role of the internet pornographic industry in contemporary societies that profoundly rely on communication technologies and innovation, or what Jodi Dean (2010) has framed as communicative capitalism. In this

© The Author(s) 2016
A. Fotopoulou, *Feminist Activism and Digital Networks*,
Palgrave Studies in Communication for Social Change,
DOI 10.1057/978-1-137-50471-5_3

chapter, my own particular interest is with the immense tensions and contradictions that characterise pornographic and feminist self-exposure practices. What is political in these practices? Feminist debates around pornography may be old, but this does not mean that they are resolved, or that there is consensus within contemporary feminist movements about how to handle such a controversial issue – especially since the appearance of self-representing porn and body art in digital media. In what follows, I offer a substantive account of the complex relationship between feminist rhetoric and the online porn market. Stemming from the biopolitical framework of network capitalism that I employ throughout the book, my main argument is that queer and feminist identities are becoming increasingly diffused. The abundance of new forms of porn that are circulated online mark the biodigital space that is produced between worlds of bodies (bioart, postporn) and informational worlds of bits and connections. As a political space, this has been conceptualised as non- or anti-reproductive, in the sense that it opposes the social reproduction of heteronormativity, mainly from within queer studies and predominantly in the work of Edelman (2009). Other radical scholarly work in queer studies and 'postporn politics' (Stüttgen 2009) has embraced bioart and sex weblogging, also as expression forms of embodied resistance to a norma-tive sexual order (Diefenbach 2009). Porn studies literature (Attwood 2009; Paasonen 2007; Williams 2004), an important field that is acutely aware of how necessary feminist and queer approaches are in internet studies, is ambivalent about new forms of pornography such as internet porn.

It is tempting, when thinking about pornography and feminism, to reduce the matter to a pro-/anti-debate. So a key task here is to first attempt to untangle some of the past and present feminist debates on pornography. Then, we must deal with how some new forms of queer/feminist pornographic expression have sought to create utopian, struc-tureless spaces where economic alternatives to capitalism are being tested (Lovink 1992; Jacobs 2010). In these cases, sexual politics and the politics of pornography have enabled participants to engage directly with impor-tant political concerns. But as we will see later in this chapter, the political space demarcated by feminist and queer porn production is inherently paradoxical. This is because it is characterised by content generation that is guided by neoliberal discourses of consumer choice and sexual agency, in the same way as any other porn production that is not specifically feminist or/and queer agenda.

Sex Wars and Pornography Debates

In the past, fierce debates between feminists revolved around the political importance of pornography as a form of communication that objectifies women (Cornell 2000; Rubin 1993). This long history of second-wave feminist struggle over representation shapes the prevailing contemporary feminist positions around pornography and sex work: pornography is still today understood as a symbolic form of violence against women, and a symptom (or sometimes, cause) of rape culture (Hayes et al. 2016; Horeck 2014; Mendes et al. 2016; Rentschler 2015). But how have feminist in the past tried to overcome the connection between representation and symbolic violence?

In the 1970s, the Women's Liberation Movement challenged existing representations of women in film and aimed to produce alternative positive images of older, black women or women in work-related roles (Becker et al. 1981: 1). Laura Mulvey's (1989 [1975]) canonical text *Visual Pleasure and Narrative Cinema* argued that, to put it simply, in narrative film the figure of the woman invokes fear of castration, and for this female characters were symbolically punished. Beyond the problem with the representation of women in general, many lesbian cinema producers tried to address lesbian invisibility, in particular, in conventional cinema and as a result of this, they created a cinema where lesbian experience was central (Becker et al. 1981). The British experimental cinematographist Barbara Hammer (1993) is a key figure in this field, as she combined radical content and form in order to express lesbian experience. Hammer's cinema is playful and interesting – despite perhaps her essentialist clingings to an autonomous lesbian sexuality – because she linked abstraction with physical sensations, such as pain and perceptual pleasure.

In the 1980s, the polarisation between the urge to explore sexual issues vs. 'shock, righteousness and prohibitiveness' (Ardill and O'sullivan 1989: 128) was intense in feminist and lesbian cultures. At the time, the first lesbian-feminist sadomasochist (S/M) texts were published in the USA. In the UK, respectively, the first public screening of the film *She Must Be Seeing Things* (Mclaughlin 1987) stirred considerable discussion.[1] Together with the S/M anthology *Coming to Power* (Rose and Samois 1982) and Joan Nestle's (1987) *A Restricted Country*, these filmic and critical texts presented key opportunities to revisit lesbian-feminist discourses about sexual issues, beyond censorship and pornography (see Ardill and O'sullivan 1989). Pornography as a genre however, and not just the representation of explicit scenes, was a vastly divisive object. Some feminists were critical of the way it was produced, while others were critical of porn itself. Anti-pornography campaigns in the UK attracted the attention of Labour Party MPs (Assiter and Carol 1993: 9), and surprisingly, not as much that of right-wing moralists. But some feminist theorists and producers sought to 'generate debate and criticism of sexist images' (Rodgerson and Wilson 1991: 17) rather than ban explicit content altogether. One account of this is Lynne Segal's (1992) distinction between fantasy, as a primary setting for desire, and real life; she argued that pornography produced by women producers, such as Candida Royalle of *Femme Productions*, could empower women's sexuality by creating non-phallic symbols.

The years since the 1990s saw a conceptual and activist move in queer feminist politics from questions of gender to those of sexuality as the primary site of oppression. At this time, various media texts and artists pushed the boundaries of what was acceptable in feminist cultures as well as in lesbian and gay communities. Key examples here are photographers Della Grace (later Del Lagrace Volcano) and Tessa Boffin, who published sexually explicit photography and stories, including S/M and butch/femme themes, in the magazines *Quim* ('for dykes of all sexual persuasions')[2] and *Serious Pleasure*. Consider that this was a time when display of pornographic material was restricted to licensed shops (Healey 1996). Another important figure, Volcano (1991) contributed to a production of 'radical anti-gender narratives' (Armstrong 1999: n.p.) by documenting the underground dyke-culture. Volcano's photography offered a challenge to some of the prevailing politics of feminism at the time, in the sense that, as Reina Lewis noted,

> SM is not politically correct in many circles (and indeed SM sees its job as being to challenge the hegemony of feminist moralities) and is often opposed to the critical activity of feminist theorists. (1994: 90)

Other expressions of the queer art scene were Suzie Krueger's Clit-Club[3] and the first London drag-king club, Club Naive.[4] This brief and partial history of the 1990s queer scene illustrates how feminist queer culture and queer politics engaged extensively with key debates around porn and visual representation; it is therefore unacceptable to neglect their contributions in shaping how we think about these issues today.

Post-porn, Posthumanism and Queer Negativity

Many things have changed since London's dyke-culture in the 1990s. Today, there is a wealth of porn-related production run by women, including radical and sex-positive weblogs and microblogs on platforms such as Twitter, Instagram and Tumblr. At the same time, the direct involvement in the porn industry of women who are in some way informed by feminism means that the focus of previous debates has also shifted. To illustrate here this shift, I will examine radical sex art practice in digital culture that can be thought as an expression of a 'postporn' movement. This practice takes both the form of a direct critique of mainstream, commercial pornography and of pornographic practice. Postporn describes an era of practices within digital visual culture that comprise of art and porn production, and often directly or indirectly comment on the exploitative conditions of pornography. They can be art performance, self-pornographic selfies, gender-queer porn and porn produced by women – and although generically distinct, there is little point in differentiating between them for my purposes. Think for example of Della Grace, who appeared in photographs and also provided audio narratives that accompany the models and their photographs. Another key performer is Annie Sprinkle, whose shows have been interpreted as reclaiming control over the sexualised body (Schneider 1997).[5]

There is significant traffic between the academy (feminism and queer studies), artporn, sex weblogs, online amateur porn networks and commercial porn. Although, largely, postporn conferences happen in academic or art spaces, they are increasingly organised in conjunction with commercial porn producers, as is the case with Berlin PornFilm Festival. Other expressions of this movement include weblogs, especially those of US-based bloggers who, in some cases, have worked in the sex industry and consider themselves to be sex educators. For example, Violet Blue[6] named her weblog *Open Source Sex* (*tinynibbles.com*), with allegedly 4 million readers a month, 'for the intersection of technology and sex, and the free-flowing information exchange of the open source software movement' (Violet Blue 2011). 'Postporn' in this case thus refers to an earlier era of pornographic cultural production (the porn industry of the 1980s/1990s), but it also importantly makes a case for the altered ways of understanding the body, technology and 'the human'.

Conceptually, postporn performance and politics have been influenced by posthumanism. To be sure, discourses of posthumanism/posthumanist emerge from various theoretical fields, including the humanities and feminist STS. For instance, Rosi Braidotti (2008: 178) uses the term 'posthuman' in order to contest the phallogocentric, white, male, property owning and standard-language speaking citizen, which is connoted by the name 'human'. In the same volume, *Bits of Life: Feminism at the Intersections of Media, Bioscience and Technology*, Karen Barad (2008: 172–173) defines posthumanism as 'a commitment to accounting for the boundary practices through which the "human" and its others are differentially constituted' – rather than an account of the human as 'he'. Meanwhile, in the collection *PostPornPolitics* (Stüttgen 2009), where texts originate from a postporn symposium in Berlin with the same name, the engagement with posthumanism is largely about the body and technologies as extensions of the body.

An important theoretical perspective that links queer studies, and queer porn specifically, to posthumanism was developed by Lee Edelman (2009). Edelman's (2004) primary thesis of queer negativity in his book *No Future* questioned what he calls 'reproductive futurism', in other words how heteronormativity reproduces through discourses and positive feelings such as hope. For Edelman, queer is fundamentally antisocial; it is the 'structural embodiment of resistance to normativity' (2009: 35). He goes as far as to argue that queer is an opposite to the very concept of 'the human' in liberal democracies. Following that line of thought, and through an engagement with Alain Badiou's theory of the event, Edelman conceptualises queer porn as a posthuman *event* that disrupts social order and unified identity. So if we ask, what is political in queer porn, according to Edelman it is how it operates as a disruption of the 'normal', expected flow of ordinary, heterosexual and reproductive sex. Queer sex and queer porn are darker, not hopeful or looking into the future for the possibility of creating life, or maintaining continuity with the past. Of course, this account has two problems: first, it denies that queer families can be political; and second, it views politics as inherently anti-social and disruptive. Other scholars in the same volume also make a case for posthumanism and postporn politics as interruptions. Katja Diefenbach (2009), for instance argues, 'the political cannot be substantialised in something subjective, human, or living' (p. 4). And Beatrice Preciado's (2002) *Contrasexual Manifesto* is given multiple references. The latter has a cult status, not only in this collection, but also broadly in queer performance cultures around Europe (Total Art Journal 2011). It advocates the use of dildos, as non-reproductive sexual organs, through a series of exercises that aim to 'resist the normative production of the body and its pleasures' (Total Art Journal 2011: 2). The emphasis on non-reproduction, both biological and social, is what connects these texts, and a wider preoccupation for queer porn writers. But what happens to digital reproduction? How does the replicability of digital texts, including queer porn streamed or downloaded online, inform this debate? This remains underdeveloped, but porn production is inextricably linked to digital and internet technologies, as I explore later in the chapter.

Postporn as a movement, through its conceptual engagement with posthumanism, makes a case about the politics of events or situations, and the contingency of unpredictable connections. It should thus come as no surprise that anthologies and essay collections theorising postporn and netporn branch out of face-to-face conferences and meetings.[7] Katrien Jacobs, an academic and performer, has framed the organising of 'Porn Ar(t)ound the World Festival', and other postporn events more generally, around Hakim Bey's (1991) early vision of *Temporarily Autonomous Zones* – which can be loosely understood as utopian structureless sites where people meet and try out economical and sensual alternatives to capitalism (see also Lovink 1992; Jacobs n.d). As one of the 'C'lick Me' conference organisers, Marije Janssen (2010), told me in an interview, artists and participants in radical sex workshops share concerns about how 'to sustain, control the body or force/morph the body'. They use their own bodies and bodily material as sites of intervention. For Janssen (2010), the encounters of BDSM-pornographers, like WARBEAR of 'Phag Off', and bio-artists, like Kira O'Reilly, constitute attempts to challenge disembodied learning and networking. For example, Kira O'Reilly employs performance, video and installation to consider the body as a site for narrative threads of the personal, sexual, social and political. Her work *inthewrongplaceness*, for instance, was a four-hour session with the artist lying and moving naked across the carpet with a dead pig. The overlap of pleasure, homoeroticism and suffering are similarly prevalent in the work of live artists Ron Athey, Franco B, Orlan and Stelarc, where bodies are the site of technological intervention. Although such performances cannot be considered as explicitly radical sex activism, they create situations in which both human and non-human bodies, and their boundaries, are questioned.

With the invocation of postporn performers for the use of prosthetic parts and artificial organs, the body is re-signified in ways that undermine the binary construction of material/immaterial. It has been well documented how the body is a multi-dimensional site of struggle. Critical frameworks such as corporeal feminism, as developed by Elizabeth Grosz (1994), have shown how the body, both as materiality and as a symbol, is a central resource for culture. When it comes to art practice, digital devices function as prosthetic extensions of the human sensorium in the vein once described by Marshall Mcluhan (1964) – as *aides de memoire*, as the means of contact and engagement with the world. Beyond overwriting the biological body then, postporn practices construct a hybridised body, which resembles a mechanical and informational body.

I.K.U.

Shu Lea Cheang's 2001 film *I.K.U.*,[8] a Japanese sci-fi porn film, is a good example of a postporn/artporn filmic text that explores the interchange between ideology, digital technologies, pleasure and cultural politics in inventive ways. It is about a virtual human named I.K.U. Coder. The synopsis of the film reads as follows:

The GEN-XXX I.K.U. Coders were superior in their hard-drive bodies, and at least equal in insatiability, to the programming engineers who created them. I.K.U Coders were used in the night-world as XXX data hunters, in the orgasmic exploration and sexualisation of other couples. After a non-stop sexing journey by a GEN-XXX I.K.U. Coder team in the night-world, Coders were declared full data – ready for retrieval. Special data collectors – I.K.U. RUNNER UNITS – had orders to fuck to retrieve, upon detection, any full data I.K.U. Coders. This was not called love, this was called sex (I.K.U., The Movie 2009).

The creator Shu Lea Cheang is a multimedia artist exploring themes of trans, postporn, cyberfeminism,[9] and *I.K.U.* has caught the attention of scholars from various disciplines. In Eve Oishi's (2007) reading, Cheang's feminism gathers around the concept of the transhuman quality of the body, how it is a site of information extraction. New forms of consumerism offered by the internet also result in seeking pleasure, so commodity culture has for Oishi redefined sexual pleasure. Cheang's cyber-art, including *I.K.U.* (2000), deals with issues of exploitation of physical bodies for erotic pleasure and natural resources, through commercial and technological networks. In this sense it can be considered as anti-capitalist and compatible with ecofeminism (Oishi 2007). From a cyberfeminist perspective, Yvonne Volkart (2002) has argued that sex in *I.K.U.* shapes the cyborg's subjectivity; it embodies digital technologies and dissolves gender dichotomies.

To me, *I.K.U.* is contradictory. It is unclear, for example, how *I.K.U.*, by not showing human bodies having sex, is different from mainstream male porn or how Cheang's identification as trans – actually transcends both hetero – and homonormativity (Sullivan 2001). I agree that the idea of 'natural' sexuality is questioned in *I.K.U.*, however, I am sceptical as to how far the hardcore pornographic elements of Cheang's work 'transform the value of these images from a simple monetary one to other forms of exchange and utility' (Oishi 2007: 24). The use of porn conventions in *I.K.U.* has been interpreted as a feminist critique of corporate mainstream porn (Jacobs 2003). For Jacobs (2003), the 3D digital penis that is shown in the film intentionally depicts women as coders, hence active agents, in contrast to how they are represented in Japanese porn (i.e. forced sex). Seen in this light, the 'pussy as matrix'[10] (2003: 202) is for Jacobs the alternative to male-centred pornography. To me, the interesting aspect of the film is how it tackles themes of extraction and commodification. Orgasms in the film are selected, collected, categorised and transformed into information that can subsequently be sold. Here, Cheang develops a critique of capitalism's ability to modify emotions and sensual responses into data. 'The human body in IKU, she argued, is a gigabyte hard drive' (Sullivan cited in Oishi 2007: 30). Cheang's project thus addresses the female body as the site of information extraction in new biotechnological and digital economies, which is a key preoccupation in my work. Although in *I.K.U.* the critique concerns the commodification of immaterial and intangible labour, like those in arousal and orgasm, the notion of capitalist extraction relates to feminist biopolitics and reproductive technologies, as we saw in the last chapter, and to digital-free labour that we will see in the next section of this chapter.

Artporn, Postporn and the Question of the Political

Beyond the critical questions that the art piece poses though, participation in such events is thought as a disruptive or political act according to postporn scholars. I am wary of conceptualisations of such events as auton-omous zones or political by default. But undoubtedly, being at a specific time and place with certain people gives participants an opportunity to make up their minds about whether the performances are art or porn, pleasurable or obscene, or both. Of course, as Marije Janssen (2010), co-organiser of *Netporn politics* conferences, explains, festivals and conferences host audi-ences already aware of the production, distribution and content differences between artistic and commercial explicit material. Today the blur between high art and low pornography has meant that arousal in public has become part of legitimate culture, as Linda Williams notes in the epilogue of *Hardcore* (1989). Art audiences may in fact manifest their cultural capital by discussing the thin line between art and pornographic object in such events, and by also negotiating in private what is acceptable to feel at a corporeal level. After all, we make meaning within social contexts and affective encounters, and the affective elements of these spaces and networks are crucial. This is because, as I outlined in Chapter 1, affective experiences like pain, arousal, joy or shame can motivate us to act politically (see Ahmed 2002; Grosz 1994; Munt 2008). As Debra Ferreday (2009: 37) argues, reading of belonging and community through theories of affect allows a clear understanding of how the personal and the political intersect. Here I argue that it is the affective elements that constitute feminist and queer digital networks that engage with pornography potentially political.

Despite their uncontested affective and bodily manifestation however, it seems to me that the fantasy of erasing the reproductive body in postporn texts, practices and networks flirts narrowly with the traditional fantasy of disembodied information. In Western culture, information has been largely assumed to be immaterial (Hayles 1999). It is also the case that practices extending the body with the use of technologies are tied up with anxieties about the status of the body in exceedingly technological environments. Does the materiality of the body still matter in informational networks? Is the pornographic body still a body when it is streamed online and viewed on tiny screens? Does technology in the form of prosthetic organs empower the pornographic body and protect it from the ill-effects and potential risks of over-exposure? Digital technologies make the body malleable, uncertain. With social media in particular, the individual, a concept that was stabilised in Western thought during the Enlightenment, has come to be understood as the constantly visible body. There is indeed a generalised uncertainty about social norms and relationships in the context of commodification and increased visibility – think for instance of the AIDS crisis, anorexia and all sorts of addictions, including the recently invented sex-addiction in films such as *Shame*. So, postporn networks are yet an example that illustrates the ambivalence of queer and feminist politics of sexuality about embodiment in relation to online networks and informational capitalism (another example on this but this time in relation to reproductive politics is discussed in Chapter 4).

SELFIE FEMINISM AND WEBCAM PRINCESSES

The recent explosion of online selfies and sexting in digital culture also raises fundamental questions in relation to what online exposure and surveillance mean for women and girls, and what role feminist critique can play in addressing these developments. Of course, selfies are not always pornographic, but as Ann Hirsch wrote, 'Whenever you put your body online, in some way you are in conversation with porn' (cited in Darling 2013: n.p.). I will add that you are also in conversation with feminism, and feminism is in conversation with both. An example here is Molly Soda, a contemporary self-proclaimed 'webcam princess' who emerged from the early days of Tumblr and has done explicit photography. A recognised digital artist who exhibits mostly self-portraits today, Soda identified as a feminist in an interview for the magazine Dazed: 'It's exciting to see other girls around the world doing cool things, like helping each other and just existing really. That's activism in itself' (Mosey 2015). In a piece for Open Space of SFMOMA, Sarah Burke (2016) re-introduced a term that has been variously used in the last years, fourth-wave feminism and described it as:

> basically, a reiteration of third-wave feminism that takes into account the experiences of 'digital natives' and the extent to which online platforms provide space for promoting gender equality. It's a form of feminism that appreciates the complicated intersectionality of Beyoncé's *LEMONADE*, but ultimately finds itself in a camp more particular to Millennials (and less so to black and brown experience).

Soda's identification as a feminist assumes this fourth-wave feminism of empowered young women who share digital content online, and redefine what being looked-at means. As is the case with postporn and sex-positive or feminist porn, Soda's (and other selfie artists) artistic and cultural content creation engages actively with feminist debates, which illustrates again the on-going exchange between contemporary feminism, porn and selfies.

Feminist writing has framed the debate around selfies and sexting in terms of vulnerability and agency, focusing, on the new demands put on young women to express sexual agency and choice in neoliberal societies (see Gill-Peterson 2015; Bay-Cheng 2015). Women who take selfies and particularly those who take sexually explicit or auto-pornographic selfies (comprising of text or image, or combining both) have of course been seen as passive victims of many other more active agents, be it their own narcissism or men who manipulate them to engage in the practice, and they have been patronised as ignorant of both systemic sexism and the affordances of digital technologies.[11] The media discourse about selfies and self-shooters has thus re-articulated key cultural anxieties about the female body and girls in particular. But for many feminist scholars, selfies, seen both as technological objects and as cultural practices, have enabled new types of feminist discourse, primarily intersectional and anti-racist, to circulate in the public realm. There are many examples of so-called 'selfie feminism' (mainly post-2013), mostly hashtag feminist campaigns that have erupted on Twitter, such as #feministselfie, @loveyourlines (that celebrated stretchmarks), or the feminist challenge 'Girls not plucking their armpit hair' hosted on Sina Weibo, the Chinese platform similar to Twitter (see Minh-Ha 2015; Pisani 2015). A study of the 'not safe for work' [NSFW] bloggers (Tiidenberg 2014; Tiidenberg and Cruz 2015) has noted the specificity of issues of control, power and the gaze in the Tumblr community and argue that self-shooters are empowered through their practices.

However, I do not find it productive to recreate the binary 'victimisation vs. agency'. First of all, selfies are still a form of self-branding for microcelebrities, or people who aspire to become one, in a consumerist era. But even if they become one, their profits will surely be less than the profits of platforms (Van Dijck 2013). Platforms operate on the basis of algorithms, which guides what trends and what gets 'liked' in social media (Gerlitz and Helmond 2013). In this sense, the commodification of the images, and the self-branding of these images and their creators severely undermines the political undercurrent of 'selfie feminism'. We also need to consider that today, as we live *in* and *with* the media, social media have become fundamentally normative, in terms of our everyday expectations of privacy (or loss of, for that matter), but also in terms of our exposure to diverse types of bodies and bodily experiences. One would just have to exclaim at the amount of natural birth videos available publicly on YouTube to realise that the aura of our most private moments has been lost forever in the era of streaming digital reproduction. Therefore, I remain principally unconvinced about the subversive elements and disruptive power of media practices such as explicit selfies. But let us see how the technological terrain has shifted in the last years, and with it our understandings of bodies.

'PORN 2.0' AND AFFECTIVE LABOUR

In the last few years, changes in porn production and distribution have changed how we understand the body in digital culture. Arguably, the increased commodification of the female body in online porn has shaped what we find acceptable, in terms of representation, and how we define porn. Historically, different practices and debates about porn have emerged alongside the development of media technologies and forms of distribution (Attwood 2009; Nikunen and Paasonen 2007; Williams 2004). Thus, in the 1970s, film-based pornographic material became increasingly available due to the proliferation of VCR format technologies and the consequent drops in the cost of producing porn (Williams 1989). Today, the conditions offered online are favourable both for small ventures and amateurs, and for larger companies. E-commerce appeals to new entrants due to low entry costs, while it constitutes a safe environment for exhibitionism (Cronin and Davenport 2001). Additionally, the diversity of distribution channels offered online allows adult entertainment companies to sidestep some of the legal and socio-cultural constraints that are related to traditional markets, such as exporting to countries with different regulations. Today, many sex-positive porn producers such as Erika Lust, venture to use social media platforms like YouTube as a distribution channel, but stumble upon its terms of use and policy against nudity and explicit content (Cafolla 2016). Of course, censorship in social media platforms is a controversial issue, especially if one considers the multiple hashtags that are banned on Instagram for no obvious reason (e.g. the hashtag 'photography'), other than the flooding of content after a generic user search. Instagram has strict policies around nudity and users become increasingly inventive in terms of hashtag use in order to surpass censorship.[12]

But more generally, if we look at the internet, from its early days to recent 'Web 2.0' technologies, we can see how media economies have been transformed (Paasonen 2010) and are still changing, in terms of both content generation and distribution. Growing technological convergence has made it possible for companies to distribute pornographic material in different formats, online and offline (Nikunen and Paasonen 2007). In the 1990s, slash[13] fandom cultures moving from VCR technology to the internet were enthusiastic about the possibilities for sharing porn material (Penley 1997: 115–116). Later, Web 2.0 enabled online amateur and peer-to-peer (P2P) porn exchanges (Jacobs 2007; Slayden 2010), an advancement that was even heralded to constitute non-commercial counter sub-cultures and 'hacti-vism'[14](Jacobs 2007: 49). For Slayden, the proliferation of user-generated and alternative porn[15] constitutes a field where consumer tastes and demands change too quickly for the commercial porn industry to catch up with and, in this sense, signals a democratising 'power of consumers' (2010: 66). However, such approaches do not take into account the reliance of late capitalism – and the porn industry in particular – on the extraction of value for 'free' and 'affective' labour.

'Affective labour' broadly describes the unpaid investment of time, voluntary work and connections of users. One important account of user labour and its role in new information economies can be found in Terranova's *Network Politics* (2004), who builds upon the Italian Autonomist Marxist tradition – mainly Hardt and Negri (2000) and Mauricio Lazzarato (1996). As we saw in the last chapter, in *Empire*, Hardt and Negri (2000) use the term 'affective labour' as a conceptual tool for historical materialist analysis, and to describe intensities, emotions, internalised feelings and the production of meanings in technological capitalism.[16] Meanwhile, Lazzarato (1996) reflects on the production of informational commodities across classes and uses the term 'immaterial labour' to label it. As I discussed in the previous chapter, new forms of gendered and sexualised labour, such as unpaid domestic work done by women, are a key pre-occupation in recent feminist scholarship. This work attends to emerging global inequalities recorded in the expansion of the care sector for instance (Fortunati 2007; Ehrenreich and Hochschild 2003), whereas others have focused on reproductive labour. Terranova additionally offers fundamental insight into the links between unpaid technocultural production such as ordinary everyday user content and contemporary capitalism. According to her framework, digital economy[17] channels new types of collective labour that have developed due to the expansion of cultural industries. 'Free labour' is thus the,

> excessive activity that makes the [i]nternet a thriving and hyperactive med-ium ... – a feature of the cultural industry at large, and an important, yet unacknowledged, source of value in advanced capitalist societies. (Terranova 2004: 73)[18]

The creation of online communities and content is one of the ways this type of labour manifests. Terranova's (2004) critique of 'gift-economy' paradigms and open-source communities additionally points out how such phenomena do not signal the 're-emergence of communism within the cutting edge of the economy' (p. 77). This is particularly relevant if we consider how online commercial porn sites today (like *SuicideGirls.com*) employ gift values to make profit. Several empirical projects have attended to these new forms of labour in the last few years, from the study of early social networking websites, such as *Myspace* (Cote and Pybus 2007), to netporn amateur production in Web 2.0 (Mowlabocus 2010; Paasonen 2010). Amateur and postporn networks and exchange cultures do not operate outside economics and their autonomy is questionable; after all most companies have now adopted freeware/shareware strategies. In fact, as I will explain in the last part of the chapter, such commercial sites and amateur networks claim to engage in queer, feminist, 'postporn' politics. But what exactly is political here?

To get to that question, I will close this chapter with a case that illustrates how, in digital networks, the discourses of authenticity, productivity and individuality shape a post-feminist understanding of porn, which legitimises digital pornographic practices and, at the same time, creates new audiences. My argument is that although lesbian and gay porn existed in earlier media forms, it is the increased availability of social media platforms, and digital media more broadly, that present a fundamental challenge to the very notion of feminist porn. Promoting 'participation', feminist and queer porn producers invite viewers and porn consumers to engage as politically aware and sexually empowered subjects.

NOFAUXX

There is a wealth of alternative netporn producers, sex-columnists and bloggers, such as *Anna the Nerd* and like Audacia Ray of *Waking Vixen*, Violet Blue of *Open source sex* and Melissa Gira Grant of *sexerati*. These medium-specific brands combine 'geeky' identities, in that they address topics such as the internet and new media technologies in combination with sexual politics, feminist politics and porn production. They combine feminist themes and entrepreneurial practices.

nofauxxx.com is a queer and women-owned porn production company that claims a feminist identity[19](from now on *Nofauxxx*). *Nofauxxx* is appealing as a research site especially since it has been considered a 'business with a *sexually correct* spin' (emphasis in the original) (Pasquinelli 2010: 4) that destabilises gender binaries (Jacobs 2007). My analytical focus here is interview material, Frequently Asked Questions and Mission

Statement sections of the websites, which operate as the main branding and promotional venues for the company.

The company belongs to the growing field of female-to-male (FTM) and gender-queer pornography, which has been thought to involve 'a variety of ethnicities, body sizes and cultural expressions, the unifying element being their sexplicit transmasculine content' (Waxman 2006: 1). Courtney Trouble, the creator of the *Nofauxxx* company, presents herself as a 'queer feminist pornographer/photographer' (2009) and the website features 'performers of all genders, sizes, races, sexual orientations'. On the front webpage, the project announced 'alternative girls, hot boys, transfolk, gender queers, and real life couples' (Nofauxxx 2011) in 2011, and five years on, 'gorgeous women, femmes, couples, dykes, bois, trans women, punks, sex workers, ftms, queer men, bbws, lesbians, husbands, gender queers, gender fuckers, bisexuals, queer porn stars, people of color, people of size, people of love, people of indie porn' (Nofauxxx 2016). The website uses upbeat web graphics, which differentiates it stylistically from many websites of dyke porn or women-owned production companies, which seem to still follow a 1990s web aesthetic. Moreover, the website features 'alternative' models of punk, emo and other subcultural styles, with characteristic piercings and tattoos.

The company's emphasis on alternative concerns both content and production practices. There is an assumption, therefore, that audiences are familiar with mainstream porn *genre* conventions, such as iconography, themes, narratives and style.[20] In lesbian and dyke porn, for example, the 'authentic' butch and the butch/femme dyad have served to legitimise lesbian porn (and sexuality for that matter) as distinct from heterosexual porn (Butler 2004). However, Nofauxxx promises to transgress these generic boundaries of both dyke and hetero porn, beyond the introduction of new iconographic signifiers – beyond representation.

It additionally claims to challenge the norms of the pornographic industry by inviting users to become producers. For example, the membership link is labelled 'Join the Revolution', which evidently is an attempt to give the website some political edge. Similarly, in an interview to *Ssspread Magazine*, the owner of *Nofauxxx* provides a personal narrative that presents becoming a porn producer as emancipatory.

> By 2003 I had been working as a phone sex operator full time for a few years and was feeling a burnout associated with being men's fantasies all day.

I thought that working on my own fantasies and my own body as a source of fantasy would be a great way to work through those emotions. The photos of my friends and myself ended up being the first incarnation of *NoFauxxx. com*. (Trouble cited in *Plato* 2009)

In this narration, conditions of work characteristic of neoliberalism (e.g. the blurring between producer and consumer, commercial relationships and friendship, working time with leisure time) are translated specifically for the context of online porn companies. The revolutionary tone characterises all of the company's websites, blogs and magazines and builds Trouble's brand persona as a 'queer porn icon' (Trouble 2010). The extent to which the marketing strategies of the website correspond to the actual conditions of labour are beyond the purposes of this study. It is nevertheless useful to note the case of *SuicideGirls.com*, an allegedly post-feminist production company, which claimed to empower women models through their work (see also Magnet 2007). However, it has been reported that 40 models have exited the man-owned company due to its exploitative and misogynistic attitudes (Mccabe 2005). Empowerment discourses, and the focus on choice and agency, are therefore often used to mask the exploitative conditions of sex work. Sex labour (alongside 'care') operates within such wider neoliberal frames, and as socialist feminist critiques have identified, women and other vulnerable social groups are the first ones to be pulled into 'flexible' work (see Weeks 2007).

But we must also deal with the exoticisation of queer sexuality in the Nofauxxx pages. Queer sexuality has often been overemphasised as intrinsically revolutionary in queer studies (Berlant 1995; Berlant and Warner 1998). In Berlant's early work Live Sex Acts (1995), the visibility of queer sexual practices fundamentally disrupts heteronormativity. Maybe this was the case before internet connectivity became the standard way of communication though. Publicising non-reproductive sexual practices arguably had a different symbolic power then. In its early days, the internet was also frequently declared a queer liberation front. Marchetti (2001) wrote, for example, that 'breaking into cyberspace parallels breaking out of the closet, and queer space opens up as invitingly as does screen space' (p.413). These celebratory accounts of the internet as a space for queer visibility and existence have perhaps now lost their poignancy, although as research shows, social media are still critical in the coming-out process of queer youth who live far from urban centres (Gray 2009). What is important here, however, is how queer sexuality, tied up with the exotic, is used in branding Nofauxxx as inclusive and diverse. The all-inclusive casting plays a central role in this branding strategy:

> We draw from many sources to create a community of varied identities. We do not take gender, size, race, or any other consideration into consideration when choosing our models. We do not have quotas or any ideals about what a porn star should look like. Additionally, we do not separate the girls from the boys on our site, as many of our models fall somewhere in between. (Nofauxxx: Mission 2016)

The discourse of authenticity and queer visibility in a way create an artificial scarcity. Although scarcity is used primarily in connection to raw natural material resources, it is relevant to digital products and their cost in the creative industries, not least because of digital replicability. Artificial scarcity strategies are standard market features in the internet era (Berry 2008; Mansell 1999; Sullivan 2016). In the process of claiming visibility, queer alt porn constructs the queer and trans body as a new 'other' and re-inscribes hierarchies of sexualities. Audiences are here invited to glimpse into the lives of queer bodies as if they hide unexplored pleasures. As Sarah Ahmed (2004) reminds us, this is not new: queer social life has often been presented as an unchartered territory of pleasure to be discovered by heterosexual audiences, just like the pleasures of colonialism that were out there, to be discovered by the British empire. What *Nofauxxx* markets as proof of authenticity, and as a political project of including marginalised sexual and 'race' identities, performatively produces these identities and concurrently legitimises them as pornographic objects. In this way, *Nofauxxx* becomes the author and the brand that responds, through its media production, to the porn industry, as if the inequalities that characterise it are indeed the inequalities and issues of queer politics. Celia Lury (2006) suggests that the emergence of a brand signifies the transformation of the author function precisely because all media are nowadays meta-media. *Nofauxxx*, in this light, becomes the brand that answers to the demands of a world emerging in mediation, 'a world that increasingly comes into existence as media' (Lury 2006: 94).

The producer goes as far as to construct the ideal consumer group for these non-normative productions: those who perceive porn to have cultural and political value – 'the subversive, political, and inquisitive crowd' (Trouble 2010). Trouble promotes the company as an active component of a queer community whose lifestyle includes queer and trans politics. In other words, her address to 'queer folk' interpellates a niche notably different to that of the lesbian and gay mainstream consumer – and advises what politics involves for them. What is different in this case from the mainstream address of LGBT consumers in cultural places such as the theatre, clubs or books today is the incorporation of political values that in fact emerged within queer theory and the trans movement. 'Queer folk' in Trouble's address is thus not just LGBT-identified consumers, but porn users with a specific political and cultural capital, which is what differentiates them from users of other dyke and lesbian porn websites.[21]

'Real' (and not virtual or fantasy) in pornography principally signifies different-to-porn-stereotypes. Since the early days of the internet, real-core pornography has been produced and exchanged online by amateurs and particularly within BDSM and fetish communities, who this way surpassed commercial porn imperatives (Messina 2009). In scholarly work, the real/virtual binary as it played out in assumptions of fluidity and performativity in queer studies has been criticised early on (see Wakeford 1997; O'riordan 2007). And the blurring between 'real' and 'representation' has a prominent place in porn studies (Attwood 2010). In queer porn platforms like *NoFauxxx* these same debates seem to be re-articulated but now as meta-concerns; in other words, with an obvious *awareness* of both the particularities of networked media environments (their hypermediacy) and the political correctness for middle-class LGBT identified people.

> When I started NoFauxxx.Com, one of my main goals was to create an all-inclusive community, where anyone would feel comfortable expressing their desires through film. (Trouble, in Plato 2009)

As is also the case with selfies feminism, participation is a basic rhetorical tool for alt porn sites like Nofauxxx. Being able to express oneself and participate signals a key component and mode of engagement of digital culture. Participation is the optimistic and very often uncritical version of unpaid user-generated content, which disguises the power dynamics and economics of platforms. Producing more content, more images, and enabling more visibility of a wider range of bodies that have traditionally been underrepresented, such as trans or black, is by itself not necessarily empowering for marginalised communities and subjectivities. As Dean (2009) argues, the belief that informational abundance is democratising is a fantasy that largely what drives neoliberal subjects today. Paired with the neoliberal myth of sexual agency, choice and empowerment, the *fantasy of more* (more content, more choice) essentially defines digital culture. In *Nofauxxx* (but also in the photos of body hair in Soda's work), the digitally mediated glimpse into the scarce, hidden, untold characteristics of 'real' bodies and sexual practices, and the invitation to participate, problematically fuses commodification, feminist/queer politics and internet myths.

CONCLUSION: FROM EXPOSURE TO POLITICS

Selfies, alt queer porn, postporn and artporn are different media forms but all create and cultivate a relationship between pornography, consumerism and sexuality politics, with the use of digital technologies. This has key consequences for the cultural meanings of production and consumption of porn; as practices of generating and exhibiting online self-pornographic content become mainstream and are claimed to be empowering by fourth-wave feminists or 'selfie feminists', we observe a re-articulation of the key themes of feminism and queer politics. Definitions of the pornographic object emerge through the communicative acts of the producers and the participants or viewers.

But these practices are often deeply problematic; as we saw in the example of Nofauxx, in the process of claiming visibility, online queer alt porn sites construct the trans body as scarcity in a capitalist economy, and as a new colonial 'other' in a moral economy, and as a result, re-inscribe hierarchies of sexualities in informational capitalism. Along with processes of self-surveillance in postporn networks, and the integration of capitalist trait of abundance, under the guise of gift exchange, open community and participation, digital porn culture produces new commodifiable connections and subjectivities of consumption. As I argued, affective labour is commonplace in these networks and events, which further legitimises capital value extraction from queer bodies, women's bodies and FTM bodies. Far from announcing digital networks of queer/feminist porn production and dissemination to be liberatory spaces in a simplistic manner, I indicated how they essentially open up new markets in academic, artistic and other settings.

But what is then, if at all, feminist here? Be it with visual texts posted online, or physical art pieces, bodily self-exposure enables a space where people share a sense of corporeal vulnerability, regardless of whether they claim that the practice empowers them or not. Beyond the surveillance aspects of social networking and mobile media, our bodies are invariably constituted in the public sphere. As Judith Butler writes, they are already exposed to touch, gaze and violence and thus are by default vulnerable (Butler 2004: 26). When Butler (2004: 27) argues about imagining community in her account of loss and violence, she refers to the threat to life itself; one could argue that the threat of the exposed, sexualised body in digital media merely implicates representations and symbols. This is risky territory, especially because, as I have already registered earlier in this chapter, and in Chapter 1 with reference to rape culture, the debate about whether violence against women and pornography operate on the plane of the symbolic or the material remains unsettled in feminism. However, if we consider affect as an intrinsic component of making meaning, we could begin thinking of vulnerability in digital technologies and in the porn industry as it operates biopolitically, beyond the binaries of material/representational, symbolic/real, body/mind. These are then new forms of biodigital vulnerability that I introduced in Chapter 1, which can be politically empowering when their public recognition enables feminist actors to assemble, to mobilise and perform forms of political subjectivity.

Queer and postporn networks are aware of their subordination and their vulnerability due to exposure – which differentiates them significantly from heterosexual amateur porn cultures. It is because of this awareness that they can create politically enabling networked connections. But while 'digital natives' of selfies and the social media age seem to be revisiting issues of visual representation, visibility and the gaze, those who practice postporn and body art examine different sets of questions, such as the role of technological innovation in extending and redefining the boundaries of bodies and gender. These explorations of who we are and how we can live with digital media technologies reflect, as I argued in the first part of the chapter, deep anxieties about what constitutes authenticity and individuality, and at a wider scheme, what it means to be human. As embodied practices, postporn art, feminist selfies and queer/feminist porn are performed through digitally connected networks and are essentially driven by the neoliberal discourses of abundance, consumer choice and sexual agency. At the same time, they attempt to articulate a political response to the new forms of governmentality that have appeared because of technoscientific acceleration. It is this inherent contradiction that constitutes pornography an exemplary illustration of how bodies and technology remain today entangled in ways that make biopolitical feminist critiques more necessary than ever.

NOTES

1. *She Must Be Seeing Things* was the first film that explicitly addressed internal tensions in lesbian relationships. Critical engagement with the film revolved around heterosexuality and dominant codes of representation. The director Sheila McLaughlin (Butler 1993) thought that her work treated lesbian anxieties about heterosexuality in ways similar to the publication *On Our Backs* (1984) in New York. Certain scenes stood as a dramatisation of the debates which evolved within lesbian communities at the time, namely around sex-positive attitudes and S/M as opposed to 'vanilla' sex (Quimby 1991).

2. *Quim,* edited by Sophie Moorcock and Lulu Belliveau, was a forum for artists of the avant-garde scene where, according to Armstrong (1999), for the first time 'lesbians and female sex-adventurers could experiment and play freely without being exposed to the straight gaze'.

3. This was a fetish dyke club-mainly leatherwear, featuring an alternative *cabaret* with a short sexual performance where the artists would use hard-core techniques, like real bodily fluids (Armstrong 1999).

4. See also the feature film *Dandy Dust*, bringing together sexual club perfor-mance spaces and cyborg fantasy. This is an experimental film which involves the character Dandy Dust who is a 'split-personality cyborg of fluid gender' (BFI Mediateque 2011).

5. In *Public Cervix Announcement*, audiences were invited to look at the performer's vagina using a flashlight (See Sprinkle 1998).

6. She has been named *Wired*'s 'Faces of Innovation' and interviewed, in between others, at *The Oprah Winfrey Show*. She has also published *The Smart Girl's Guide to Porn* and given lectures at UC Berkeley.

7. For example, such events are the 2005 conference *The Art and Politics of Netporn* and the 2007 *C'lick Me* festival, both in Amsterdam (See Jacobs 2007). Also the *Vivo Arts School for Transgenic Aesthetics Ltd*, the *Berlin Porn Festival*, the *Porn Ar(t)ound the World* in KCNona, Mechelen, Belgium, *Artivistic* in Montreal, and *Arse Electronika* in San Francisco. Other central events are *Impakt Festival Utrecht*, 2006 and 2008, *Post Porn Politics Symposium,* Berlin, October 2006, *Pinched Festival,* Amsterdam, June 2008, *Ladyfest* Dusseldorf, August 2008, *Rated X Festival* Amsterdam, January 2009, *Stoute Dromen* (Belgian feminist) Festival Antwerp, October 2009, *TurnOn Artivistic Festival,* Montreal, October 2009, *Viva la Vivo,* Amsterdam, November 2009.

8. The word 'iku' is slang for 'having an orgasm' in Japanese.

9. Her net installation works are in the permanent collections of the Walker Art Center, Minneapolis, NTT[ICC], Tokyo and the Guggenheim Museum: Bowling Alley, 1995; Buy One Get One, 1997; and Brandon, 1998–1999. Her net installation 'Milk at 56 KB Bastard TV' and the porn cast call

installation 'Fluid' for Norway Detox festival (2004–2005) explored issues of exploitation of sexual bodies and visibility in digital economies and post AIDS societies.

10. The film uses a subjective view, the 'pussy point of view', which is deep in people's vaginas.

11. See, for instance, the November 2013, *Jezebel* published an article under a headline that declared, 'Selfies Aren't Empowering: They're a Cry for Help' (Ryan 2013).

12. For a list of absurd hashtag bans, see: http://madamenoire.com/508687/banned-instagram-hashtags/7/.

13. 'Slash' is a fiction genre that depicts same-sex romantic or sexual relationships between fictional characters, for example from *Star Trek* (see, e.g. the website *slashfic.org*).

14. Hacktivism is 'hacking for a political cause…a policy of hacking, phreaking or creating technology to achieve a political or social goal' (METAC0M 2003).

15. He uses 'Porn 2.0' (2010: 55) to refer to user sites like Xtube and YouPorn.

16. Many scholars have been critical of neo-Marxist (often also referred to as 'post-operatist') economic theories (Weeks 2007) and have commented on Negri and Hardt's renunciation of empirical research.

17. 'Digital economy' broadly refers to the emergence of computer networks, informational economies beyond the internet and forms of labour which have developed in relation to the expansion of cultural industries (Terranova 2004: 79).

18. I agree with Terranova in her understanding that we experience the world as members of relations, but I am sceptical about her discussion of informational politics, especially in regards to how exactly affect produces relationships and leads to action. How can this potential be actualised in ways that change the conditions of work for sex workers, for example, or other precarious gendered workers in the informational age of porn? Such issues remain unaddressed.

19. An examination of the visual content offered by porn websites alongside audience analysis could complement my study, but are beyond my scope. Here I am interested in the company and website branding prior to registration.

20. In heterosexual porn, for instance, these conventions include bodies enhanced by plastic surgery, maximum visibility of genitalia and male ejaculation as evidence of pleasure.

21. This is not to say that *NoFauxx* offers something radically different – other sites like the *Crash Pad Series*, featuring primarily dykes but increasingly 'today's blurred gender lines and fluid sexualities', follow similar marketing tactics.

BIBLIOGRAPHY

Ahmed, S. (2002). The contingency of pain. *Parallax, 8*(1), 17–34.

Ahmed, S. (2004). Affective economies. *Social Text, 22,* 117–139.

Ardill, S., & O'sullivan, S. (1989). Sex in the summer of '88. *Feminist Review, 31,* 126–134.

Armstrong, R. (1999). Cyborg film making. *Cybersociology Magazine* 5. http://www.cybersociology.com/files/5_cyborgfilmmaking.html. Accessed 10 December 2010.

Assiter, A., & Carol, A. (1993). *Bad girls and dirty pictures: The challenge to reclaim feminism.* London: Pluto Press.

Attwood, F. (2009). *Mainstreaming sex: The sexualization of Western culture.* London: I. B. Tauris.

Attwood, F. (Ed.) (2010). *porn.com: Making sense of online pornography.* New York: Peter Lang.

Barad, K. (2008). Living in a posthumanist world: Lessons from Schrödinger's Cat. In A. Smelik & N. Lykke (Eds.), *Bits of life: Feminism at the intersections of media, bioscience, and technology* (pp. 165–176). Seattle, WA: University of Washington Press.

Bay-Cheng, L. Y. (2015). The agency line: A neoliberal metric for appraising young women's sexuality. *Sex Roles, 73*(7), 279–291.

Becker, E., Citron, M., Lesage, J., & Rich, B. R. (1981). Lesbians and film. *Jump Cut: A Review of Contemporary Media, 24–25,* 17–21.

Berlant, L. (1995). Live sex acts (parental advisory: Explicit material). *Feminist Studies, 21*(2), 379–404.

Berlant, L., & Warner, M. (1998). Sex in public. *Critical Inquiry, 24,* 547–566.

Berry, D. M. (2008). *Copy, rip, burn: The politics of copyleft and open source.* London: Pluto Press.

Bey, H. (1991). The temporary autonomous zone, ontological anarchy, poetic terrorism, the hermetic library at hermetic.com. http://hermetic.com/bey/taz3.html. Accessed 29 July 2009.

BFI Mediateque. (n.d.). Dandy Dust (1998). http://ftvdb.bfi.org.uk/sift/title/518244. Accessed 10 January 2011.

Braidotti, R. (2008). The politics of life as bios/zoe. In A. Smelik & N. Lykke (Eds.), *Bits of life: Feminism at the intersections of media, bioscience, and technology.* Seattle: University of Washington Press.

Burke, S. (2016). Crying on camera: 'Fourth-wave feminism' and the threat of commodification. http://openspace.sfmoma.org/2016/05/crying-on-camera-fourth-wave-feminism-and-the-threat-of-commodification/.

Butler, A. (1993). She must be seeing things: An interview with Sheila McLaughlin. In M. Gever, P. Parmar, & J. Greyson (Eds.), *Queer looks:*

Perspectives on lesbian and gay film and video (pp. 368–378). New York: Psychology Press.

Butler, J. (2004). *Precarious life: The powers of mourning and violence*. London: Verso.

Cafolla, A. (2016). Erika Lust speaks out about SFW porn film banned by YouTube. http://www.dazeddigital.com/artsandculture/article/31309/1/erika-lust-speaks-out-about-sfw-porn-film-banned-by-youtube.

Cheang, S. L. (2000). *I.K.U.* [Tokyo]. Oaks, PA: DVD UPLINK Co. Distributed by Eclectic DVD Distribution.

Cornell, D. (Ed.) (2000). *Feminism and pornography*. Oxford: Oxford University Press.

Coté, M., & Pybus, J. (2007). Learning to immaterial labour 2.0: MySpace and social networks. *Ephemera: Theory and Politics in Organization, 7*(1), 88–106.

Cronin, B., & Davenport, E. (2001). E-rogenous zones: Positioning pornography in digital economy. In P. K. Nayar (Ed.), *The new media and cybercultures anthology*. Chichester: Wiley-Blackwell.

Darling, J. (2013). Performance GIFs 7: Jennifer Chan. [online] n. p. http://rhizome.org/editorial/2013/jun/11/performance-gifs-7-jennifer-chan/. Accessed 2 December 2016.

Dean, J. (2009). *Democracy and other neoliberal fantasies: Communicative capitalism and left politics*. Durham, NC: Duke University Press.

Diefenbach, K. (2009). Fizzle out in white: Postporn politics and the deconstruction of fetishism. In T. Stüttgen (Ed.), *Post, porn, politics: Queer-feminist perspective on the politics of porn performance and sex-work as culture production [symposium, reader]* (pp. 25–32). Berlin: B_books.

Edelman, L. (2004). *No future: Queer theory and the death drive*. Durham, NC: Duke University Press.

Edelman, L. (2009). Unbecoming: Pornography and the queer event. In T. Stüttgen (Ed.), *Post, porn, politics: Queer-feminist perspective on the politics of porn performance and sex-work as culture production [symposium, reader]*. (pp. 33–46). Berlin: B_books.

Ehrenreich, B., & Hochschild, A. R. (2003). *Global woman: Nannies, maids, and sex workers in the new economy*. London: Granda Books.

Ferreday, D. (2009). *Online belongings: Fantasy, affect and Web communities*. Bern: Peter Lang.

Fortunati, L. (2007). Immaterial labor and its machinization. *Ephemera: Theory and Politics in Organization, 7*, 139–157.

Gerlitz, C., & Helmond, A. (2013). The like economy: Social buttons and the data-intensive web. *New Media & Society, 15*(8), 1348–1365.

Gill-Peterson, J. (2015). Sexting girls: Technological sovereignty and the digital. *Women & Performance: A Journal of Feminist Theory, 25*(2), 143–156.

Gray, M. L. (2009). *Out in the country: Youth, media, and queer visibility in rural America*. New York: NYU Press.

Grosz, E. A. (1994). *Volatile bodies: Toward a corporeal feminism*. Bloomington: Indiana University Press.

Hammer, B. (1993). The politics of abstraction. In M. Gever, P. Parmar, & J. Greyson (Eds.), *Queer looks: Perspectives on lesbian and gay film and video* (pp. 70–75). New York: Routledge.

Hardt, M., & Negri, A. (2000). *Empire*. Cambridge, MA: Harvard University Press.

Hayles, N. K. (1999). *How we became posthuman virtual bodies in cybernetics, literature, and informatics*. Chicago, IL: University of Chicago Press.

Hayes, R. M., Abbott, R. L., & Cook, S. (2016). It's her fault student acceptance of rape myths on two college campuses. *Violence against Women* doi: 10.1177/107780121663014

Healey, E. (1996). *Lesbian sex wars*. London: Virago.

Hess, A. (2015). The selfie assemblage. *International Journal of Communication*, 9, 1–18.

Horeck, T. (2014). #AskThicke: 'Blurred lines', rape culture, and the feminist hashtag takeover. *Feminist Media Studies, 14*(6), 1105–1107.

Jacobs, K. (2003). Queer Voyeurism and the Pussy-Matrix in Shu Lea Cheang's Japanese Pornography. In C. Berry, F. Martin, & A. Yue (Eds.), *Mobile cultures: New media in queer Asia* (p. 201). Durham, NC: Duke University Press.

Jacobs, K. (2007). *Netporn: DIY web culture and sexual politics*. Lanham: Rowman & Littlefield.

Jacobs, K. (2010). No Title. Interviewed by Aristea Fotopoulou [Skype Voip recording] Brighton – Hong Kong, 7 February 2010.

Jacobs, J. (n.d.) Black magic doesn't swallow: My response to the porn ar(t)ound the world festival, Libidot. http://libidot.org/blog/columns/. Accessed 29 April 2011.

Janssen, M. (2010). No title. Interviewed by Aristea Fotopoulou [email] Brighton – Amsterdam. 26th April 2010.

Lazzarato, M. (1996). Immaterial labour. In S. Makdidi, C. Casarino, & R. Karl (Eds.), *Marxism beyond Marxism*. London: Routledge.

Lewis, R. (1994). Dis-graceful images: Della Grace and lesbian sado-masochism. *Feminist Review, 46* (Sexualities: Challenge & Change (Spring, 1994)), 76–91.

Lovink, G. (1992). Interview with Hakim Bey: Breast-to-breast anarchy. Internet archive, community audio. http://www.archive.org/details/InterviewWithHakimBeyAboutBreastToBreastAnarchy_345. Accessed 29 July 2009.

Lury, C. (2006). 'Contemplating a self-portrait as a pharmacist' a trade mark style of doing art and science. In M. Fraser, S. Kember, & C. Lury (Eds.), *Inventive life: Approaches to the new vitalism* (pp. 93–110). London: Sage.

Magnet, S. (2007). Feminist sexualities, race and the internet: An investigation of suicidegirls.com. *New Media Society, 9*, 577–602.

Mansell, R. (1999). New media competition and access the scarcity-abundance dialectic. *New Media & Society, 1*(2), 155–182.

Marchetti, G. (2001). Cinema frames, videoscapes, and cyberspace: Exploring Shu Lea Cheang's fresh kill. *Positions: East Asia Cultures Critique, 9*, 401–422.

Mccabe, J. (2005). Suicide girls' exodus. F-Word [blog]. 23 November. http://www.thefword.org.uk/blog/2005/11/suicide_girls_e. Accessed 3 August 2011.

Mclaughlin, S. (1987). *She must be seeing things.* [VHS] New York: First Run Features.

Mcluhan, M. (1964). *Understanding media: The extensions of man.* Cambridge, MA: The MIT Press.

Mendes, K. D., Keller, J., & Ringrose, J. (Forthcoming 2016). Speaking 'Unspeakable Things': Documenting Digital Feminist Responses to Rape Culture. *Journal of Gender Studies.*

Messina, S. (2009). *Realcore: The digital porno revolution.* http://www.sergiomessina.com/realcore/index.php. Accessed 10 August 2011.

METAC0M. (2003). What is hacktivism? copyleft: The thehacktivist.com. http://www.thehacktivist.com/whatishacktivism.pdf. Accessed 16 August 2011.

Minh-Ha T. Pham. (2015). 'I click and post and breathe, waiting for others to see what I see': On #feministselfies, outfit photos, and networked vanity. *Fashion Theory, 19*(2), 221–241.

Mosey, A. (2015). The digital artist who's dating a teddy bear. http://www.dazeddigital.com/artsandculture/article/24362/1/the-digital-artist-who-s-dating-a-teddy-bear.

Mowlabocus, S. (2010). *Gaydar culture: Gay men, technology and embodiment in the digital age.* Aldershot: Ashgate Publishing.

Mulvey, L. (1989 [1975]). *Visual and other pleasures.* Bloomington: Indiana University Press.

Munt, S. (2008). *Queer attachments: The cultural politics of shame.* Aldershot, England: Ashgate.

Nestle, J. (1987). *A restricted country.* Ithaca, NY: Firebrand Books.

Nikunen, K., & Paasonen, S. (2007). Porn Star as Brand: Pornification and the Intermedia Career of Rakel Liekki. *The Velvet Light Trap, 59*(1), 30–41.

Nofauxxx. (2011). http://nofauxxx.com/tour-2. Accessed 16 August 2011.

Nofauxxx. (2016). http://nofauxxx.com/tour-2. Accessed 16 July 2016.

O'riordan, K. (2007). Queer theories and cybersubjects: Intersecting figures. In K. O'riordan & D. J. Phillips (Eds.), *Queer online: Media technology & sexuality* (Vol. 40, pp. 13–30). New York: Peter Lang.

Oishi, E. (2007). 'Collective orgasm': The eco-cyber-pornography of Shu Lea Cheang. *Women's Studies Quarterly*, *35*, 20.

Paasonen, S. (2010). Labors of love: Netporn, Web 2.0 and the meanings of amateurism. *New Media & Society*, *12*, 297–1312.

Panayotakis, C. (2003). Capitalism's 'dialectic of scarcity' and the emancipatory project. *Capitalism Nature Socialism*, *14*(1), 88–107.

Pasquinelli, M. (2010). The masochism of the commodity form: Queer porn and the fine art of paradox. In ICI, Desiring Just Economies conference, Berlin, 26–26 June 2010. http://matteopasquinelli.com/docs/Pasquinelli_Commodity_Masochism.pdf. Accessed 1 August 2011.

Penley, C. (1997). *NASA/TREK: Popular science and sex in America*. New York: Verso.

Perelman, M. (1993). Marx and resource scarcity. *Capitalism Nature Socialism*, *4*(2), 65–84.

Pisani, L. M. (2015). *Performative embodiment and the self(ie): Defining the political feminist self(ie)*. MA major research paper. Toronto: York University Toronto.

Plato, C. (2009). Getting in Trouble: The founder of nofauxxx doesn't fake it. Interview with Courtney Trouble. $pread Magazine. http://www.spreadmagazine.org/Trrouble5.1.html. Accessed 10 March 2010.

Preciado, B. (2002). *Manifiesto contra-sexual: Prácticas subversivas de identidad sexual*. Madrid: Pensamiento Opera Prima.

Quimby, K. (1991). *She Must Be Seeing Things* Differently: The limits of Butch/Femme. In K. Jay (Eds.), *Lesbian Erotics*. New York: New York University Press.

Rentschler, C. (2015). #Safetytipsforladies: Feminist twitter takedowns of victim blaming. *Feminist Media Studies*, *15*(2), 353–356.

Rodgerson, G., & Wilson, E. (1991). *Pornography and feminism: The case against censorship by feminists against censorship*. London: Lawrence & Wishart.

Rose, B, S. A. M. O. I. S. (1982). *Coming to power: Writings and graphics on lesbian SM*. Boston: Alyson.

Rubin, G. (1993). Thinking sex: Notes for a radical theory of the politics of sexuality. In H. Abelove, M. A. Barale, & D. M. Halperin (Eds.), *The Lesbian and gay studies reader*. New York: Routledge.

Ryan, E. G. (2013). Selfies aren't empowering: They're a cry for help. *Jezebel* November 21. http://jezebel.com/selfies-arent-empowering-theyre-a-cry-for-help-1468965365. Accessed 25 March 2014.

Sassen, S. (2011). Fabricating scarcity. Scarcity exchanges. University of Westminster. Backdoor broadcasting academic podcasts 13 June. http://backdoorbroadcasting.net/2011/06/saskia-sassen-fabricating-scarcity/. Accessed 23 June 2011.

Scheirl, H. (1999). Dandy Dust., S.l. Millivres Multimedia.

Schneider, R.. (1997). *The explicit body in performance*. London: Routledge.

Segal, L. (1992). Sweet sorrows, painful pleasures: Pornography and the perils of heterosexual desire. In L. Segal & M. McIntosh (Eds.), *Sex exposed: Sexuality and the pornography debate* (pp. 65–91). London: Virago.

Slayden, D. (2010). Debbie does Dallas again and again: Pornography, technology, and market innovation. In F. Attwood (Ed.), *porn.com: Making sense of online pornography*. New York: Peter Lang.

Sprinkle, A. (1998). *Annie Sprinkle: [post-porn modernist: My 25 years as a multimedia whore]*. San Francisco: Cleis Press.

Stüttgen, T. (2009). *Post, porn, politics: Queer-feminist perspective on the politics of porn performance and sex-work as culture production [symposium, reader]*. Berlin: B_books.

Sullivan, J. L. (2016). Software and Artificial Scarcity in Digital Media. *The Political Economy of Communication, 4*(1), 66–84.

Sullivan, M. (2001). Lesbographic pornography. In A. Koivunen & S. Paasonen (Eds.), *Conference proceedings for affective encounters: Rethinking embodiment in feminist media studies*. Series A, no. 49. Turku: University of Turku. http://www.utu/hum/mediatutkimus/affective/proceedings.pdf.

Terranova, T. (2004). *Network culture: Politics for the information age*. London: Pluto Press.

Tiidenberg, K. (2014). Bringing sexy back: Reclaiming the body aesthetic via self-shooting. *Cyberpsychology: Journal of Psychosocial Research on Cyberspace, 8*(1), Article 3. Doi:10. 5817/CP2014-1-3.

Tiidenberg, K., & Cruz, E. G. (2015). Selfies, image and the re-making of the body. *Body & society*. 1–26. doi: 10.1177/1357034X15592465.

Total Art Journal (2011). The Contra-sexual Manifesto (expert). http://totalartjournal.com/archives/1402/the-contra-sexual-manifesto/. Accessed 17 July 2010.

Trouble, C. (2010). Courtney Trouble: Queer porn icon. http://courtneytrouble.com/about. Accessed 17 July 2010.

Van Dijck, J. (2013). *The culture of connectivity*. Oxford: Oxford University Press.

Violet Blue. (2011). Open source sex [blog]. http://www.tinynibbles.com/. Accessed 10 January 2011.

Volcano, D. L. (1991). *Love bites: Photographs*. Boston, MA: GMP; Distributed in North America by Alyson Publications.

Volkart, Y. (2002). Technics of cyberfeminism: Strategic sexualisations. Between method and fantasy. In C. Reiche & A. Sick (Eds.), *Technics of cyberfeminism. <mode=message>*. Bremen: Thealit. http://www.obn.org/reading_room/writings/html/strategic_sex.html.

Wakeford, N. (1997). Cyberqueer. In S. Munt & A. Medhurst (Eds.), *The lesbian and gay studies reader*. London: Cassell.

Waxman, T. (2006). GenderFluXXXors uncoded: An FTM supornova performance Interview with Katrien Jacobs. Sexxchange Salon, Hong Kong. http://www.tobaron.com/genderfluxxxors.html. Accessed 17 July 2011.

Weeks, K. (2007). Life within and against work: Affective labour, feminist critique and post-fordist politics. *Ephemera: Theory and Politics in Organization, 7*, 233–249.

Williams, L. (1989). *Hard core: Power, pleasure, and the 'frenzy of the visible'*. Berkeley: University of California Press.

Williams, L. (Ed.), (2004). *Porn studies*. Durham: Duke University Press.

CHAPTER 4

From Egg Donation to Fertility Apps: Feminist Knowledge Production and Reproductive Rights

Reproductive rights have been a key issue for feminist politics. From the first publication of *Our Bodies, Ourselves* by the Boston Health Book Collective in 1970, the feminist health movement has formulated a wider critique of technoscience. Scholars in the field of social studies of science and technology have argued that gender and sexuality relations of power get reproduced through technoscientific practices (see Fox Keller 1995; Haraway 1997; Harding 1991; Thompson 2005). Networked media and digital technologies are, at the same time, means of communication about gender relations, and themselves technoscientific practices. I have shown in the first three chapters that the fundamentally new structures and practices of digital and networked media transform how feminist activists think and fight for gender equality. This may not necessarily echo the hopes of writers who pronounced Web 2.0 and digital media inherently democratic. But it certainly carries the promise and potential for a new mode of feminist politics.

So what happens when digital media and reproductive politics intersect? What form might contemporary feminist interventions take and how does the intersection between biological and digital shape these interventions? In this book, my argument builds on the premise that acceleration of digital and biotechnological innovation and increased connectivity change the material conditions of life and introduce new forms of governmentality that are specific to women and queer people. My claim is that, in this

© The Author(s) 2016
A. Fotopoulou, *Feminist Activism and Digital Networks*,
Palgrave Studies in Communication for Social Change,
DOI 10.1057/978-1-137-50471-5_4

context, feminism and queer activism are today characterised by deep contradiction, because they attempt to articulate a critique of these new forms of governmentality, while using these technologies. In this chapter, I focus on feminist biopolitical projects that aim to address reproductive technologies.

When it comes to reproductive rights and the online digital world, a key question is how to continue thinking about political representation in a space that has shifted and mutated because of the prominence of digital networks and technoscience in our everyday lives (Terranova 2004). Indeed, if we consider the global flows of information, services and bodies, it becomes increasingly difficult to even imagine a unified feminist political identity – a 'we' – in this context. This is not because issues such as patriarchy, egg donation, and abortion have ceased to matter or been resolved in an era of online petitions and campaigning. But such a space has also allowed for celebrity feminism to flourish, which inspires a mode of engagement that is, at the same time, apolitical and protectionist towards the world's 'others'. Think for example of Angelina Jolie's announcement in 2013 of her decision to undertake preventive double mastectomy after genetically testing for *BRCA1* gene.[1] The publicity of this decision not only caused a surge in information seeking about cancer online (Noar et al. 2015), but there was also a significant rise in the demand for BARC1/2 testing and for risk reducing mastectomies in the UK between 2012 and 2013 (Evans et al. 2014). Although Jolie's public narrative and subsequent moves have been celebrated as a public health education initiative (Nisker 2013), they have importantly legitimised the voice of risk and fear, and the importance of self-care and self-responsibilisation around health and wellbeing.

Beyond the Angelina Jolie effect, we observe today an unprecedented proliferation of health information, from both official and alternative media sources. Forums such as Mumsnet and popular mobile phone apps like Kindara enable the development of new layperson knowledges around one's own health and well-being – and as has been noted signify new maternal subjectivities and cultural understandings of pregnancy (see Longhurst 2009; Tyler 2011). Using gadgets for self-tracking and quantification have become standard practices for many. Quantification involves monitoring fitness, sleep, mood or other kinds of everyday physical activity and logging it using spreadsheets, mobile phone applications, or the interfaces provided by commercial or custom-made wearable electronic devices. Women track periods and reproductive function. In this context, women adopt a multiplicity of identities when engaging with such material online, not only in relation to genetic testing and preventive measures for female cancers, but also with reproductive rights and fertility policies. For example, as we will see later in the chapter in relation to egg donation, they can be patients, potential donors, engaged consumers or responsible citizens. Such identifications reformulate, rather than transgress, gendered and other social expectations, for example those associated with caring and being a mother. This complex process of identification and negotiation of roles indicates the complexity of articulating political voices in relation to reproductive technologies and science today.

As we will see in the second part of the chapter, women's organisations are variously positioned within a spectrum of feminist identities ranging from grassroots to feminist bioethics. My argument here is twofold: first, even though online and mobile technologies offer the possibility to facilitate new modes of engagement with biomedical knowledge and, therefore, the production of new political realities, their use also raises some critical social, political and ethical questions around, labour and exploitation, data ownership and power at the intersections of the digital and biological. Second, I argue that contemporary feminist biopolitical publics and activist projects can be better understood in relation to embodied, material practices of knowledge production, mutual learning and self-experimentation with digital media and smart technologies.

I start here from the premise that it is impossible to think about the digital and contemporary media more generally as merely technological, or even as simply 'social' – an attribution certainly popular today. As was also the case in the previous chapter, when thinking about the global flow of informational bits and the tracking and sharing of data, we need to also encompass the live and fleshy bodies that generate such data, for example in the case of fertility tracking; or the bodies of pregnant women who search the web for information about the life or termination of their foetus. Highlighting materiality not only of bodies but also of settings and practices that tend to be regarded as online or digital and therefore somehow immaterial or 'virtual' by default is a feminist task in itself. My task in this chapter is to revisit the notions of biopolitics and biopower in order to accentuate the biodigital vulnerabilities created in relation to reproductive technologies, by focusing on the example of fertility policy and egg donation. Drawing from examples in the UK and internationally, I examine in the second part of the chapter the communicative acts through which feminist networks are constituted. Knowledge making is at the heart of these communicative acts that cut across academic/grass-roots, online/offline, and national/local spaces, whilst challenging these boundaries. I analyse how certain feminist networks constitute alternative but credible sources of knowledge, and how they attempt to foster their credibility, and hence their capacity to speak for certain social groups. Building on Steven Epstein's (1996) exemplary work on AIDS activism, I indicate that this mediation creates the conditions necessary in order for various feminist publics to challenge official framings and perceptions of power of biomedical institutions and subsequently influence policies. Their participation in mainstream media legitimises them as representatives of affected groups in society, but as we look more closely it is clear that there are challenges. First, let us start here with a reconceptualisation of biopolitics.

Revisiting Biopolitics

The concepts of biopower and biopolitics can serve an analytical approach that recognises the centrality of digital network technologies in the regulation of social life and in the constitution of new forms of control. Reproduction has become a site of systematic intervention that is also widely accepted as legitimate – it has indeed become 'a bio-political space *par-excellence*' (Rabinow and Rose 2006: 21). Scholars from different traditions agree that biopower operates in dispersed ways (see Haraway 1997; Hardt and Negri 2000; Terranova 2004); however, there are different readings of what form politics can take in this context, or what biopolitics mean for that matter. Three key theoretical strands can help us navigate the question of biopolitics: Foucault's theorisation of biopolitical power (or biopower); Hardt and Negri's work in *Empire*; and the different feminist readings of biopower by Haraway, Braidotti and others.

In the *History of Sexuality*, Foucault (1978) traces how historically homosexuality became the pathological 'other' of heterosexuality. In his later lectures, Foucault (2008) further introduced the notion of governmentality to describe the mechanisms of neoliberal governance that directly or indirectly affect social life and individual subjectivity. Governmentality explains how social relations changed in the 18th and 19th centuries with the emergence of certain biomedical and administrative practices. Biopower appears here to be constituted by the institutions, practices and discourses of the Victorian Era, which regulated life through the control of both the personal body and the public, for instance through population control (Rose 2001). As Lazzarato's reading of Foucault underlines, this period also saw the emergence of *homo oeconomicus* in neoliberalism: 'the individual as an "entrepreneur of oneself", maximizing himself or herself as "human capital"' (2009: 111). We will see later in this chapter that this is particularly relevant when thinking about the commodification of fertility and reproduction today. What makes Foucault's theorisation invaluable is how the emergence of biopower signifies the historical transition from disciplinary societies to societies of control. But can his analysis be used to tackle technoscientific advances of the late twentieth century and early twenty-first century?

It is precisely to this historical conjuncture (the same one that this book addresses) that both Hardt and Negri's (2000) political philosophy in *Empire* and Donna Haraway's (1997) cultural study of science and technology speak. In addressing the specificity of contemporary capitalism, Hardt and Negri (2000) turn to the question of corporeal productivity. The term describes the production of life and the manipulation of affect. They read Foucault's biopower as a form of power

> that regulates social life from its interior, following it, interpreting it, absorbing it . . . Biopower thus refers to a situation in which what is directly at stake in power is the production and reproduction of life itself. (Hardt and Negri 2000: 23–24)

What this approach enables in regards to reproductive technologies is thinking about policy and biomedical intervention on women's bodies or, on an even smaller scale, their eggs and embryos. This is because it indicates how the exercise of power operates today through the interlinking of information systems (the digital) and welfare systems (the biological). Thus, although in the societies described by Foucault the differentiation between biopower and biopolitics is clear – in that biopower concerns more the interventions on the biological body, whereas biopolitics concern knowledge and technology –, this distinction becomes blurred in *Empire*. Biopower and biopolitics overlap, because interventions on bodies, populations and knowledge production are so decisively intertwined in our technologically advanced societies. In fact, for Hardt and Negri, the struggle of living labour becomes the struggle over language and technology today (2000: 406).

But what does this position mean for politics, and specifically, for how we can imagine feminist politics? Is there still space for identity politics or a politics of gender and sexuality if we accept Hardt and Negri's assertion that we are dealing with different expressions of power, implemented in the form of knowledge production, the production of gendered labour (in its most usual facets as reproductive, precarious and flexible) and the management of life and death? Terranova (2004) envisions network culture as the site of strategic and tactical struggle (p. 138) where the networked multitude emerges as a different mode of politics (pp. 152–153). Even as this approach promises to account for the social constitution of subjects in networked spaces, its commitment to 'the multitude' tells us little about the specificity of embodiment and gender.[2] Equally, although Hardt and Negri (2000) speculate that interactions between bodies in social spaces can create politics, this is always expressed through the multitude, which limits how we can speak for situated body politics around reproductive technologies.

Interlinking biological and informational systems of power, biological and digital, is perhaps a route more familiar to feminist framings before Hardt and Negri's take on biopower. I am thinking specifically here about those focusing on transgressions of feminist politics at the turn of the century. Haraway (1988) argued that, in post-industrial technoscientific capitalist societies, feminist politics should be reframed, and to this end, she proposed the overused (and more often abused) figure of the cyborg. The introduction of the cyborg not only aimed to negotiate the question of machine and embodiment but also functioned as a way out of the universalising tendencies of feminist politics at the time. Variously taken up, the cyborg metaphor has seen its most interesting application in Rosi Braidotti's writings. In Braidotti's (1994) exploration of embodiment and biotechnologies, it is precisely the aspect of the body as part of a capitalist production machine, and particularly women's bodies as biopower (in the form of genetic material, eggs, organs, foetuses), which produces new kinds of global inequalities. Braidotti's (1994) reading of Haraway's cyborg figure suggests a feminist politics that is built around this shared myth (the cyborg). But although Braidotti's take on promises to privilege the embodied subjectivity of women, as concurrently discursive, corporeal and technological, in her later works she effectively erases gendered identity altogether. This is disappointing but maybe expected, since in her reading of Haraway alongside Deleuze, Braidotti (2002) frames body and machine as symbiotic and problematically merges the human and the technological. Braidotti's (2006) later posthumanist ethical project is precisely to challenge a unified identity and to render visible how gendered, radicalised and ethnic oppression is produced through global systems of biopower. I see the validity of this project and the necessity of ethical responsibility but I think that we still need identity, in our struggles for recognition and visibility. So taking an approach quite different to Braidotti's philosophical nomadism and critique of liberal individualism, my argument here focuses on how vulnerability can be productive in addressing the question of material feminist politics and embodiment in contemporary biodigital capitalism.

Neoliberal governance is increasingly articulated through discourses of risks (see Beck 1992; Sunder-Rajan 2006; Rabinow 1999) and the mobilisation of fear (Dean 2009). This makes it important to turn risk and vulnerability around; can we make use of risk and conceptualise vulnerability in ways that empower instead of victimise women? Haraway (1997) used the metaphor of 'diffraction' to address the material/semiotic practices of science and how they can be accountable. This metaphor can be more generally applied to the production of knowledge; realities and representations need to be shaped in ways that are responsible to vulnerability. Haraway's (1997) rationale is precisely our susceptibility as embodied subjects to risk and vulnerability. I find this a more productive way of reading biopolitics and gendered embodied subjectivities. Women are at the same time political subjects and vulnerable bodies, affected by technoscientific realities produced online. But these realities are not only shaped by scientific discourse, produced by scientists and science media and geeky communication. They are also produced in participatory media, in social media, forums and user content. By sharing often very personal and intimate stories about their vulnerable, or sick, bodies, women make their bodies public. Let us think again about the case of Jolie's public campaign in favour of mastectomy. Although celebrity bodies may be thought as a priori public and subject to scrutiny by audiences and fans, such publicity can be potentially political, because it draws together an affected public – women who identify with Jolie's case.

This link between publicity and being affected by shared issues is central in John Dewey's approach to publics. Writers in the fields of science and technology studies who have also read Dewey, such as Latour and Weibel (2005) and Marres (2004, 2006, 2007) have also stressed the importance of publicity for the making of responsible technoscientific worlds. But it is Judith Butler's theorisation of precarity and vulnerability, to which return, that really helps us think about feminist politics. In Butler's (1993) *Bodies that Matter*, the materiality of discursive practices remains obscure; in

other words, it is unclear how regimes of 'truth' produce sexual differences and shape social life (Barad 2007). However, in later work, Butler
(2004) makes materiality and embodiment her key concern. As I discussed in Chapter 1, the notion of 'common corporeal vulnerability'
(Butler 2004: 42), in relation to public recognition, ethical responsibility
and political mobilisation, helps me conceptualise biodigital vulnerability
as a pre-condition for feminist and queer politics. Since the concept of
the body is constituted in public discourse (in the media for example),
Butler suggests that body politics needs to articulate a 'we' besides
ourselves and orient towards the geopolitical distribution of vulnerability. What this adds is attention to multiple responsible articulations,
debates and encounters, and the project of finding common language
to connect with one another. Butler's (2004) emphasis on the physicality, sexual passion, political rage and emotional grief in this formation (p.
24) helps us understand public recognition and the translation of this
physical vulnerability across cultures as the condition for forming international feminist coalitions.

For this project, where I am rethinking feminist subjectivity and embodiment in relation to technoscience and reproductive technologies,
Butler's (2004) interpretation of the body provides a fruitful framing of
biopolitics and biopower. The relationship between exposure, recognition
and physicality in relation to politics is fundamental for my project, precisely because public bodies today are constituted at the intersections of
information, media and other technologies of life.

But unlike other scholars who see maternal or other embodied subjectivities as limiting women's opportunities for agency (e.g. Thornham
2015), I am more inspired by projects that historicise how feminism has
actively strived to alter reprotechnologies and the lived experiences of
reproduction (see Murphy 2012). As we will see, feminists make meaning
about the role of markets, the state and supranational institutions in
regulating women's bodies, about the role of technologies in their lives
and about potential risks and opportunities, publicly, through the media,
and this includes their own experiential use of digital technologies.
Meaning – knowledge-making is for them often personal, embodied and
experiential. Thus online platforms do more than facilitate an exchange
and negotiation of ideas; they make it possible for them to mobilise for
public recognition and to develop alternative knowledge. One example that
shows how this happens is the consultation by the UK's Human
Fertilisation and Embryology Authority (HFEA) that took place in 2011.

This case helps us see the links between embodied vulnerability and politi-cisation in online networks, but also how feminist mobilisations around reproductive autonomy that operate locally or nationally connect with international feminist politics.

CHANGING REGULATIONS AND FEMINIST RESPONSES

In January 2011, the HFEA published a consultation document outlining the policies under review[3] and the Authority's position. One of the policies under review was the payment for donors. In the then legislative framework, licensed in vitro fertilisation (IVF) centres could give money to a donor as reimbursement for expenses or compensation for loss of earnings up to an overall maximum of £250 for each course of sperm donation or each cycle of egg donation (HFEA 2011), which was changed to £750 after the 2011 consultation. In contrast to the USA, and in accordance with the European Union (EU) regulatory framework, pay-ment is banned for biological donation in the UK. These policy changes signified shifts towards the US model, where compensation for genetic material is normalised and there is an established medical market in place (Almeling 2007). Changes in UK policies relating to reproduction are also informed by political shifts in the USA and the historical competition in the area of stem cell research between the two countries, at a time of changing political regimes in the UK (from a Labour Party to a Conservative–Liberal Democrat coalition government).

Variations in state regulations, which often aim to limit the use of reproductive technologies and the feminist responses to them, relate to the socio-political contexts of each country – for example, in Germany and Italy restrictive models are influenced by eugenics history and the influence of the Vatican,[4] respectively (Alkorta 2006). In the UK in the 1980s following the birth of the first 'test-tube baby', Louise Brown, in Britain in 1978, and several feminist writers expressed hostility towards what was perceived as male-controlled reproductive technology (Corea 1985; Crowe 1985; Spallone and Steinberg 1987; Wajcman 1991). By the end of the 1990s however, the payment of donors and the introduc-tion of egg sharing was the main issue of controversy for feminists.[5] Likewise, in the rest of Europe there was intense feminist involvement with the ethical, economic and social dimensions of reproductive tech-nologies. This involvement crystallised as opposition at the FINRRAGE 1985 Conference (Feminist International Network of Resistance to

Reproductive Technologies and Genetic Engineering) that drew together scholars and activists from different political terrains.[6] In the USA, and in the context of more complex political developments, what shaped regulation at a national level (when for the first time a human embryonic stem cell (hESC) was differentiated and Dolly the sheep was cloned at the Roslin Institute) was, on the one hand, the status of the embryo, and, on the other, women's reproductive rights, for instance that of access to abortion. Feminist discourses specifically around reproductive 'choice' have thus affected policy changes, but they have also been mobilised in order to legitimise certain practices of governmentality, expressed in global reproductive politics.

GENDER, EGG SCARCITY AND NEW FORMS OF LABOUR

One of the key discourses, instrumental in the way the 2011 HFEA review of payment was framed in the press, was that of scarcity of eggs for the fertility treatment of British women. On 22 August 2010, a *Guardian* article announced 'Egg and sperm donors may get £1000s in fertility plan', which was edited to read 'Egg and sperm donors may get thousands of pounds in fertility plan – Significant shift in policy aims to stop more childless couples seeking treatment abroad'. The article appeared in the Life & Style section of the newspaper, under the theme of Fertility Problems, and it was published coincidentally with an article entitled, 'Destination Spain: the rise and rise of fertility tourism – UK's waiting list for donors pushes couples abroad, where thanks to payments for donations there is no shortage'.[7] As I have discussed with reference to Dean's (2009) work on communicative abundance, and further explore in Chapter 3, the making of scarcity is a process central in capitalist economy; but within a biodigital political economy framework, such discourses of scarcity are particularly problematic. Here, abundance and its tempering (the making of scarcity) relate to creating needs and establishing the legitimacy of sourcing practices for the satisfaction of these needs. Medical professionals and women receiving IVF treatment have resorted to women mainly outside the UK for the sourcing of eggs for IVF. In a Marxist sense, egg sourcing constitutes extraction of raw material, and it often relies on the labour of poor women in non-Western countries, regulated differently in the UK. This variance in regulation, therefore, calls attention to the new forms of unequal exchange relations introduced by reproductive technologies between countries with already different economic and political powers. Marxist political economy analysis from the field of reproductive technologies has addressed these new gendered, classed and radicalised inequalities of contemporary global economies. Dickenson (2001) argues that women as a particular social group (or 'class') produce surplus through their labour in the processes of overovulation or abortion. Franklin (2007) has discussed how resource extraction ('bioprospecting') resembles agricultural technologies and engineering. Other studies (Pateman 1988; Mies 1986; Dickenson 2007; Franklin and Lock 2003; Thompson 2005) see women's bodies as generators of biovalue, property rights and as sites of exploitation. And we should not forget how scholars from an ecofeminist tradition have long connected ideas of progress with capitalism and the estrangement of humans from nature (Merchant 1980; Mies and Shiva 1993). Although different to the concepts of affective/immaterial/free labour in digital economies, the frameworks of reproductive labour developed by feminist scholars of this Marxist tradition show how central they are to global capitalism.

Perhaps more relevant here is the theorisation of 'new' forms of labour developed by Waldby and Cooper (2006; 2010), who argue that the regulation of egg donation today is inherently linked to the making of egg scarcity in the public imaginary. Waldby and Cooper suggested that the labour of egg production and vending cannot be analysed alongside other kinds of feminised labour (domestic, care, affective and sexual work). Instead, they propose the concepts of 'regenerative' and 'clinical' labour and place politics within the laboratory domain rather than everyday macropolitics. Although a discussion about labs is beyond the scope of my project here, this work is useful because it illuminates how stem cell industries capitalise on imaginaries of self-regeneration and create future markets. As Waldby and Cooper note, these future markets are increasingly concerned with issues of intellectual property, in the case of ownership of eggs or embryos in stem cell research. The regulation of intellectual rights is also a key mechanism for the making of artificial scarcity in digital media environments that are characterised by replicability and apparent abundance. Thus we can see how alienation of labour can still adequately describe both everyday materiality and digital productivity, and new developments in the lab domain. What is key for me is that women's bodies are at the forefront of biomedical and reproductive industries, just as they are in digital porn industries (Chapter 3).

In Chapter 3, I showed how queer bodies are created as artificial scarcity in online porn; here, it is important to note how the framing of egg scarcity in public discourse obscured embodiment, materiality and vulnerability, both in the sense of gendered physicality and structural conditions. For instance, both women *and* men were included in the 2011 consultation; however, egg donation involves invasive and risky procedures for women, unlike sperm donation. At the same time, the review of the payment ban arguably would create a national market of eggs that would reproduce existing social inequalities (e.g. poor women and young women in precarious employment would donate). Interestingly, Alison Murdoch, the former chair of British Fertility Society, when speaking with Lisa Jardine on Jane Garvey's *Woman's Hour* on BBC Radio 4, in favour of compensation, named eggs and sperm as 'effectively, bodily waste products', and added 'they are produced in billions, and most of them end up in the sewer' (Murdoch 2009). She stated that compensation for egg donors is only fair, since everybody else involved in the process makes money out of it. A similar position is reflected in the 2011 consultation under the principle of 'fairness' (HFEA 2011). This remarkable statement elicits understandings of women as providers of raw material in abundance and completely dismisses the invasiveness of sourcing procedures. Such official framings in mainstream media draw on liberal values of fairness and reproductive rights but disregard women's bodily vulnerability within the process of egg extraction. Although the issue here is less a matter of making value out of intellectual property (*pace* Waldby and Cooper), it still constructs a figure of women as sources of replicable, immaterial data – indeed, a cyborg figure. This opens up the question of how the proliferation of media technologies, and especially the increasing reach of the internet, has changed feminist engagement with these technologies – and particularly the power of feminist activism to influence regulation. Does the publicity around reproductive technologies and ease of networking enable new forms of involvement and solidarity? More precisely, how do feminist assemblages forming around the egg donation debates articulate a politics of biodigital vulnerability, whilst avoiding claiming that they speak for *all* women?

CONSTRUCTING CREDIBILITY AND CONNECTING LOCAL STRUGGLES

Feminist networks politicise issues around reproductive rights and technologies primarily by gaining public recognition of their significance, which necessitates building cross-cultural alliances in digital networks. In doing so, these actors attempt to establish themselves as credible sources of information on the implications of egg donation policy changes. According to Epstein (2000) scientific credibility is 'the capacity of claim-makers to enroll [sic] supporters behind their claims and present themselves as the sort of people who can give voice to scientific truths.... It is a form of authority that combines aspects of legitimation, trust and persuasion' (p. 15). Epstein (1995, 1996, 2000) identified a diversity of routes to credibility in patient activist groups in the USA, particularly around AIDS, which questioned research practices and the quality of care they received. Establishing credibility for these actors was more than a strategic use of educational degrees and institutional affiliations. As Epstein (1995) illustrates, it involved empowering laypeople's voices and legitimising these voices as credible participants in the production of certain types of scientific knowledge and, thus, democratising knowledge.

In terms of feminist activism, feminist networks have concentrated predominantly on 'risk' debates in the last decade, although there has been an on-going pre-occupation with ethics, rights and justice. During this time, several networks have formed around the world connecting local politics and the broader, open scientific literacy that challenges the material/semiotic practices of technoscience – what in other words Haraway calls 'situated knowledges' (1997: 11). Feminists have organised around global reproductive politics because of the recognition that legislative changes at a national level impact beyond the minority of Western women who use reproductive technologies (Widdows 2006). For example, laws about embryo rights affect abortion rights, whereas risky clinical practices for egg sourcing that cannot get licensed in the West are being performed in poor countries with more permissive legal frames (Cooper 2008).[8]

One example of a localised network that has produced knowledge and connected local struggles is the German Women's Forum on Reproductive Medicine, ReproKult. Founded in 1999,[9] ReproKult is:

> a nation-wide feminist network of women from the social and natural sciences, politicians, and women from professional organizations involved

with women's health and counselling centres (midwives, gynaecologists, psychologists, social workers), activist groups, and the media. (ReproKult 2005)

The network dealt with egg donation for research purposes and framed their anxiety about commercialisation on the basis of global politics and ethics. Their main concern was the risk to women's health due to the large numbers of eggs required to manufacture stem cell lines. ReproKult activists were also worried about the indirect pressure (social, cultural) on poor women to donate, especially when the terms 'donation' or 'reimbursement' essentially covered hidden commercialisation (in the case of trading eggs from Romania to the UK, for instance).

Although the critique of ReproKult has been directed at legislation governing reproductive medicine, embryo research and human genetics in Germany, their arguments share common ground with British feminist actors such as Donna Dickenson, the campaign No2Eggsploitation and the forum The Corner House. ReproKult has also had a presence in various international activist/academic meetings[10] and it has a comprehensive online database with position papers, articles, informational material and conference records, written both in English and German. Although these texts articulate a strong position, such as the 'instrumentalisation' of women's reproductive capacities for research purposes, they do operate as alternative sources of scientific knowledge about egg donation that challenge established genetic/reproductive research practices.

In the UK, a feminist network formed around the Centre for Economic and Social Aspects of Genomics (Cesagen) at Lancaster and Cardiff Universities has challenged the legitimacy of policies stemming from the 2006 HFEA consultation (Plows 2008). Scholars from this academic network criticised the framing of egg donation as reproductive freedom (O'riordan and Haran 2009). One of the key issues at this time was that of informed consent and the conditions under which human eggs could be sourced:

Women are most likely to be approached to provide some of their ova for research when they are seeking or undergoing IVF treatment...asking women to donate their eggs whilst they are concentrating on managing the IVF process is problematic. We question, therefore, what 'informed consent' would mean in this context. (Plows 2010: 143)

Others have also commented on the issue of informed consent (see Beeson and Lippmann 2006; Sexton 2005; Alkorta 2006; Dickenson 2007). 'Hands Off Our Ovaries' (HOOO) suggested a moratorium on sourcing and research until risks are known. Sarah Sexton (2005), from the organisation Corner House, indicated that ultimately structural inequalities always put women in a weaker position in consent agreements with organisational parties. The document submitted by Corner House to the HFEA review argued that there is a danger of encouraging ovarian over-stimulation practices in clinics that will aim to obtain maximum egg numbers. It advised against 'unethical and unsafe practices' and advocated 'wider consultation and decision-making process' (Corner House 2005).

By focusing on informed consent and the conditions under which human eggs could be sourced, these interventions moved the discussion away from liberal discourses of autonomy, rights, choice and the advocacy of individual reproductive rights. This critique calls for transparency in the conduct and regulation of bioscientific research and is targeted towards policymakers. In this sense, we can think of these networks as producing situated knowledge (e.g. Dickenson 2001, 2007; Haran et al. 2008, 2009; Plows 2010), perhaps not so much by aiding grassroots involvement, but rather in acting as a safeguarding structure. Still, the importance of this, and other academic networks, should not be underestimated, since they intersect with grassroots, enabling political dialogue, despite their different strategies. Feminist theorising has after all evolved hand-in-hand with reproductive technologies in the last two decades.[11]

The documents hosted online by The Corner House also encourage alliance building between different actors, by stressing the socio-political implications of egg extraction and the wider contexts within which that takes place. As an organisation, The Corner House is concerned with a broader critique of global neoliberal economic models. Reports discussing the sourcing of human eggs, mainly written by Sarah Sexton, move away from the language of reproductive rights, such as universal access to safe abortion and contraception, and the risks these practices pose for individuals, towards a framing of economic and social justice. The distance from the language of the global reproductive rights movement is not just strategic for The Corner House, but reflects a broader political position. Some of these documents have urged women's organisations to analyse the macroeconomic conditions of reproductive politics and engage with the larger agendas of social movements (Nair et al. 2004). For example, a briefing with the Women's Global Network of Reproductive Rights

(WGNRR), which researched population control policies, clarified how public health and trade policies (in the arenas of food, water, sanitation, and migration) impact on women's reproductive rights. These briefings propose that population policies, such as forced contraception and sterilisation of non-white women, are concurrently a matter of rights, markets and power. Although these papers do not draw comprehensive connections between population policies and the extraction of eggs for human embryo cloning or IVF (Sexton 1999), the circulation of information by The Corner House creates a space of political possibility by pointing less to individual risks for women's health and more to the ways these policies evolve from fundamentalist and neoliberal agendas. This is not to say that individual rights and personal bodily autonomy are not important for feminist and queer politics – it is rather to propose what Butler (2004: 27) calls 'another way of imagining community', one which accounts for the social conditions of embodiment.

Expertise has historically been held in the hands of elites who had power over the making and dissemination of knowledge. Although print and now new media technologies undoubtedly contribute to the proliferation of scientific knowledge among laypersons, making claims of knowledge remains a contested field. For example, in the case of AIDS-related knowledge, these claims have been generated out of relationships of conflict and cooperation in the USA since the early 1980s (Epstein 1996). Other networks, including those with which my empirical research engaged, have also strategically mobilised social markers of expertise, namely university affiliations, prestigious positions and academic degrees in order to foster their authority (see Chapter 5). In doing so, they have resisted a clear categorisation as academic or grassroots. Notably, Donna Dickenson and Alex Plows are both academics and involved in the informal feminist network No2Eggsploitation, which mobilised in response to the 2011 HFEA review. No2Eggsploitation was a network of activists and academics that opposed women's egg trade, and mainly published a blog and circulated leaflets at feminist conferences and gatherings.

Alex Plows, the spokesperson for No2Eggsploitation, has written about the different publics that engaged with hESC research during 2003–2007. Plows' (2010) latest book researches the emergence of feminist networks engaging with reproductive and genetic technologies, and the new forms of collective identities being shaped in this process. The book itself is a credible source of knowledge and a challenge to the figure of the 'expert' as someone 'objective' who does not get involved. For example, Plows extensively explains the use of women's eggs and processes of hESC derivation, and has engaged in public debates, appearing in BBC Radio 4 on behalf of the No2Eggsploitation campaign. Donna Dickenson is an academic working in the field of medical ethics. She is Professor Emerita of Medical Ethics and Humanities at the University of London, has coordinated research projects for the European Commission and is part of various advisory committees, namely the Royal College of Obstetricians and Gynaecologists Ethics Committee. These two public figures create a vantage point from where the No2Eggsploitation campaign can contest policymakers and other stakeholders as experts.

'WHY IS THE COMMODIFICATION OF MY EGGS SO BAD?' REPRESENTATIVENESS, CHOICE AND RESPONSIBILITY

The No2Eggsploitation campaign issued a press release and was mentioned on 17 January 2011, when the HFEA consultation launched in national media. BBC News (Gallagher 2011) quoted Alex Plows as saying:

> HFEA plans to allow financial compensation for egg donors will lead to the exploitation of young women in financial stress. These financial incentives will induce women students with massively increased debts, and others, to take serious health risks and it is inevitable that many will be harmed.

By addressing the wider public, and not just the readers of a feminist blog, the campaign assumed that their intervention had value for society at large, not only the social groups that would be affected by changes in egg donation policy.

This is also evident in the language the campaign uses in a July 2009 guest post on the *F-word* blog, posted in reaction to the announcement of the HFEA consultation, which reads, *Should people be paid for donating their eggs, sperm or embryos?* The post focused on risks for donors, such as Ovarian Hyperstimulation Syndrome, and argued these risks were the 'reason why relatively few women offer to donate eggs for others, leading to a severe shortage of donor eggs in Britain' (No2Eggsploitation 2009a). It also criticised the dishonesty of the HFEA without, however, targeting its publicity strategies. Instead, the dishonesty argument builds on an ethics basis: 'The argument that a "regulated" market in Britain is better than fertility tourism is fundamentally bad and dishonest.' Since when is it acceptable to argue that 'here is a bad thing which we have always opposed, but since people are going abroad to do it, we might as well cave in and let it happen here'? (No2Eggsploitation 2009a).

Although the *F-word* blog post – and the campaign more generally – relates the issue of egg donation to wider society, the main No2Eggsploitation campaign text addresses readers as feminists. It argued that 'feminists must speak out now to prevent this encroachment of the free market on women's bodies', and that 'feminists must make it clear that there is strong public opposition to the HFEA's plan'. The text assumes that readers have some knowledge about the state of the HFEA legislation at the time. Hence the No2Eggsploitation text invoked informed readings as well citizen responsibility for the common good. Not only the general public, but also specifically feminists were addressed as part of civil society, with duty to respond to the HFEA.

What is more, the No2Eggsploitation post referred to a character-istically British set of ethics. The authors write: 'Britain would do better to uphold its ethical principles, and resist the encroachment of the free market into every aspect of human life' (No2Eggsploitation 2009a). However, this appeal to a nationally bound set of ethics limits the possibilities for a critique that connects the 2011 HFEA policy shifts with the global traffic of eggs and women's body parts. Although they reflect values of altruistic donation and social cohesion, such positions are also risky because they may construct un-ethical 'others' which are, importantly, non-Western. As Butler (2004) suggests through her engagement with Chandra Mohanty's *Under Western Eyes*, the possi-bility of building feminist transnational coalitions depends precisely on avoiding the recreation of a homogeneous version of women and their subjectivities in relation to their locations. Thus, while the No2Eggsploitation text frames these issues in terms of the ethical collective responsibility of British citizens, my view is that an entirely different route would be more politically productive.

Although the No2Eggsploitation post was authored to highlight the themes of the ethics of the compensation and the risks of the biomedical intervention, readers approached the debate through the lens of two other themes: IVF as reproductive choice and egg trading as income source. The comments area of the blogpost suggests that the appeal to citizen responsibility is unproductive, because readers perceive egg dona-tion primarily as an issue linked to personal choice and politics. For commentators, risk, reproductive freedom, consumer choice and exploitation were central. Women who considered selling their eggs, understood going through a risky procedure as a *choice* when informed consent was in place. For instance, the commentator JDZamir, noted on the 15 October 2009:

> Yes I know the risks that are involved in egg donation. But they are my risks to take. You may class me as economically disadvantaged but that doesnt [*sic*] make my choice any less valid.

Some were sceptical of the fears that the No2Eggsploitation document expressed. One reader, pointed out on 19 October 2009: 'The issue I have with your stance here is that you are taking a very absolutist view on what is morally a grey area'. Other commentators interpreted the No2Eggsploitation intervention as a patronising rhetoric coming from a certain older, middle-class feminist perspective, which failed to grasp the materialities of poor young women. For example, Helen noted on 16 October 2009: 'Also, poor/=victim. Being poor, from a very poor family, this constantly annoys me. Seriously'; and another asked:

> Why is the commodification of my eggs so bad? And even if it is so bad surely I as a woman and feminist have the choice to make my own mistakes and successes. (No2Eggsploitation 2009b).

The comments read and respond from a diversity of positions, which the text did not explicitly address. Apart from the choice-centred responses, readers did not bring forth their feminist identity. Even though the campaign text encouraged certain readings and addressed specific feminist identities (as engaged Western citizens), readers responded as patients and consumers, and did not seem to be in antagonism with the governance of biomedicine, either as individuals or as groups. It is these identities, rather than feminist ones, which gave them a sense of empowerment and security.

Responses to the blogpost signal the difficulty in creating audience identification for issues of reproductive politics that the No2Eggsploitation campaign encountered. Collective mobilisation was hindered in this case especially because the prevailing readings brought forth liberal ideas of individual autonomy and overlooked the responsibility of the HFEA as a regulatory body. Framings of individual rights and personal responsibility communicated a negative attitude towards the view that such autonomy might not actually be in place, and this generated hostility and foreclosed further dialogue about who actually is affected by this policy shift. Forming within dominant digital culture, these reader responses can be thought to express a broader understanding of participation in digital and biomedical technologies as empowerment and individual choice (see also Chapters 3 and 5). Today, the abundance of online sources of information about health issues goes hand-in-hand with the discourses of health choice. This makes it even harder to speak of health-related social movements or draw comparisons with the AIDS activist movement, using the same terminology that applied when identity politics were prominent. Since ideas of rights, politics and the role of biomedicine are made within digital networked environments (Haran et al. 2008), it is particularly challenging for groups like No2Eggsploitation to address the multiple intersecting positions involved in the issue of payment for eggs.

However, feminist activist networks around reproductive rights and the regulation of reproductive technologies also need to differentiate from each other. For instance, the organisation The Corner House differentiates itself from earlier feminist interventions, especially those of FINNRAGE, and from mobilisations that mainly draw on the ethics arguments, such as the pro-life group Comment on Reproductive Ethics, or COREthics.[12] In sum, these biopolitical feminist networks seek to highlight how policy shifts, in particular here those proposed by the HFEA, impact women specifically and in doing so, they attempt to create new understandings about and through biodigital technologies, and the vulnerabilities these create. Differentiating from ethics framings, like those articulated by CORE, is crucial in this process. However, the strategy of differentiation for The Corner House does not involve the symbolic annihilation of other political actors – it rather upholds difference of political positions and accepts the complexity of embodiment. As the case of No2Eggsploitation shows, claiming representativeness is a complex strategy – especially when this appeals to a collective identity (British women) at the expense of another (non-British women). This exploration thus suggests that there is a need to bridge differences between feminist positions under a common articulation of women's body politics, a need to recognise cultural difference and illustrates the role of digital mediation in this process.

DIGITAL BIOPEDAGOGY AND THE QUANTIFIED SELF

Fertility policy changes as reproductive and other technologies advance, and public discourse is central to how regulation of women's bodies and reproductive capacity is understood by audiences, citizens, donors and users of reproductive technologies. But as I have argued elsewhere, the contemporary fit and healthy subject is increasingly being regulated through a series of micropractices that involve sharing one's own data via mobile apps, devices and social networking (Fotopoulou and O'riordan 2016). These are learned practices of self-care, or better termed digital biopedagogy, that teach users how to be good consumers and biocitizens. Thus to end this chapter, I would like to reflect on some new developments in the field of reproductive digital self-tracking, in order to understand feminists mobilisations as experience-based media practice, beyond the production of counter-discourse in public spaces. I will here return to my fundamental interest in practices in this book, as outlined in Chapter 1, and ask how feminist publics and activist or other political cultures can potentially come into being not just through the circulation of discourse in public platforms such as social media, but because digital technologies enable practices with social, pedagogical and political significance.

Today women track periods and reproductive function with the use of mobile apps – practices that have been widespread in analogue and that seem to be migrating into digital technology environments. One of the most popular apps is Clue, which is currently used by 2.5 million women in 190 countries. Self-tracking, as a set of practices involving various digital technologies, is clearly about self-improvement and responsibility. As such, it does flirt dangerously with a postfeminist mentality linked to freedom and choice, as well as monitoring and self-surveillance – themes that have been well discussed by both Rosalind Gill (2007) and Angela Mcrobbie (2009). In the context of digital health in particular, there is a strong link between the neoliberal citizen and healthcare under conditions of austerity – a diagnosis that many other critical scholars have made elsewhere (see Fotopoulou and O'riordan 2016; Gunnarsdottir et al. 2015). Deborah Lupton (2015), in an overview of apps and digital tools, targeted at women who monitor and manage their reproductive health, describes women as a specific version of the neoliberal citizen, responsible for her own health and well-being.

Several women-only communities, who practice self-tracking and reflect publicly upon these practices, have emerged in various cities in the USA. As sub-groups of a larger community known as the Quantified Self (QS),[13] QSXX comprises women who are concerned with visibility, or lack thereof, of women's voices and needs in the design and practice of self-tracking apps and gadgets. The network meets regularly and it comprises individuals primarily interested in their own health and well-being, but who at the same time attempt to challenge the structural gender imbalances in the tech sector. As part of the larger QS phenomenon, born in the San Francisco area, it stems from a long-lasting trend of Californian techno-utopianism, propagated by *Wired,* the leading American technological innovation magazine. Indeed, *Wired* has been central in how ideas and definitions about the QS have disseminated since 2006. With co-editor Kevin Kelly, Gary Wolf co-founder of the QS, introduced the concept of self-knowledge and large-scale data gathering. Since women have been a minority in QS groups, their issues have been marginalised. As a result, women-only spaces became a necessity.

For the Boston QSXX group, for example, a whole variety of topics is covered: hormone tracking, productivity, diet, time tracking, relationships (friendships, family, romantic), mood, fitness, etc. Few of the topics are actually women-only themes. In terms of demographics, participants are mostly women in their mid-20s to early 30s, involved in tech or technologically savvy, including many students, academics, and industry people, and occasionally a stay at home mother. To me, these QSXX groups are examples of a situated practice. As a community, they form around issues that concern and affect them, issues that make women particularly vulnerable in the context of neoliberal technoscientific assemblage. They are reflective of their privileged status as educated, techno-savvy and geeky women and from this position question masculinist design and reject apps 'mansplaining' their bodies to them. Their gatherings are storytelling opportunities, where they make sense of the information they collect, their own practices and their unequal position within the wider QS community (or 'tent' as it has been called by Nafus and Sherman). Sandra Harding (1991) has talked about making science of middle-class white men will reflect their interests and pre-occupations. QSXX are about how we need accountable technology and innovation, more women designers, and a more holistic understanding of the body. I do not mean to celebrate QSXX as a new frontier for feminism – after all it performs its own exclusions, it is largely white, middle class and heterosexual – and they are not a feminist organisation, but talking about monitoring hormones and reproductive functions potentially enables political debate around important issues of personal data and health. They may, indeed, be thought as publics emerging around 'smart' technologies – or 'smart' publics. As I have suggested elsewhere, although such publics are made, constructed, performed in culture and the media in narratives about smart technologies, and within wider narratives of economic growth, environmental crisis, economic progress and technological innovation, they could also be understood to emerge from within spaces and through practices of self-experimentation and mutual learning with digital and smart technologies (Fotopoulou 2014).

Conclusion: Biopolitical Feminist Networks

The central theme of this book is the transformation of feminist politics in a digital, always connected world. In this chapter, I examined the advancements of digital media in tandem with biomedical technologies. Today, innovation in digital technologies and computer science happen alongside biomedical advances, like the Human Genome project and stem cell research (Mitchell and Thurtle 2004; Thacker 2004). Big data are shaping our consumer profiles and our everyday environments; cars, homes and personal accessories are increasingly populated with sensors. The complex overlap of empowerment and vulnerability, in relation to the monitoring practices that harvest reproductive data, online information seeking and dialogue, makes it important to raise questions about political representation, mediation and biopower.

Feminist groups are faced with challenging negotiations of intellectual and bodily autonomy, particularly through discourses of scarcity and replicability, in relation to information and corporeality. In a biodigital context of convergence between the digital and biotechnological, reproductive and information technologies seem to mediate matters of openness of knowledge and its regulation. As the examples of the HFEA consultation and the campaigns around it show, feminist publics often form as a response to conditions of anxiety in relation to what is often assumed as given – individual reproductive freedom and liberal autonomy. We saw, for example, how audience responses in the case of No2Eggsploitation blogpost were framed around individual empowerment and choice, while the consultation material addressed women mainly as rational publics and engaged consumers. But it is important that feminist biopolitical networks organise as wider long-lasting and cross-national mobilisations around global economic tendencies, biological and genetic research and reproductive technologies. Recognition of the shared dimension of vulnerabilities posed to women and directly engaging on a critical level with the challenging conditions of biodigital technology and culture are necessary conditions for this engagement. In the examples presented here, including women communities within the Quantified Self, we saw how these networks enable knowledge-making and political involvement through the establishment of online databases, the creation of hybrid academic/grassroots spaces and practices of mutual learning and self-experimentation. I have thus argued that contemporary feminist bio-political publics and activist projects can be better understood in relation to such embodied, material practices of knowledge production with digital media and smart technologies.

As we saw, in the case of egg donation, knowledge sharing took place through online platforms and was done in less formal and more inventive ways. For instance, the ReproKult database, and the Corner House online database both functioned as archives of alternative critical knowledge about biomedical sciences. In this sense, online media aid the democrati-sation of scientific knowledge and the dissemination of campaign material. More importantly, however, digital networks mediate modes of politics, by creating spaces where dominant ideas of expertise and the dualism academic/grassroots can be challenged. Feminist networks attempt to co-produce the conditions where public and political engagement emerges by developing vertical connections between local, situated and decentralised interventions and global alliances. Central in the horizontal mode of operation of these struggles, such as mobilisation around parti-cular policy moves, is a process of differentiation between actors, which maintains the multiplicity of positions and voices and does not reduce their political identities into one single expression of feminism.

But as I argued in Chapter 1, it is not enough to reflect on what a responsible collective subjectivity means when it comes to online networks and reproductive rights, based on a model of oppositional politics of Dean (2010) or Laclau (2004). Today, reproduction, health and fitness dis-courses in policy and science media address women and activists as both sources of informational abundance, and as sources of raw bio-material. As labouring to provide tissue or data appears to be converging and to have become a condition for participation in dominant biodigital culture, feminist networks like the QSXX make meaning about these processes.

A biopolitical approach of reproductive technologies and their regulation was necessary here in order to understand how multiple embodied subjectivities and political realities might emerge. Here resides a possibility for a collective and responsible political articulation of 'we', beyond localised individual struggles – precisely because this is the terrain where claims about the universal and the personal merge. Recounting these mediations also reminds us why it is so difficult to speak today of a representational space, but for this reason so important to think of collective identities and politics in ways different to liberalism.

Feminist biopolitical networks operate on a different scale to other networks analysed in this book, but they are also distinct as a mode of engagement. Knowledge production about reprotechnologies and their regulation is central here, which indicates a historical continuity with the women's health movement. Although the means are different and arguably more digital, the pre-occupation with subjective experience and seizing control over one's body remain central.

NOTES

1. *BRCA1* and *BRCA2* are human genes that produce tumor suppressor proteins. Specific inherited mutations in *BRCA1* and *BRCA2* have been associated with an increase in the risk of female breast and ovarian cancers. Several different genetic tests that check for all possible mutations in both genes are available (see NIH 2016).
2. The multitude is Hard and Negri's (2005) conceptualisation of a network of diverse and horizontally connected actors, such as civil society organisations, who cooperate to resist social inequality in global capitalism.
3. The policies being reviewed by the HFEA included: The number of families donors can donate to; expenses, compensation and benefits in kind donors can receive for donation; donation between family members; the conditions which donors can place on the use of their gametes or embryos; the upper age limit for sperm donation, and the release of donor codes to parents of donor conceived children (HFEA 2010).
4. Britain is increasingly closer to the US model of reproductive medicine in the sense that it is very wide and permissive towards embryo research and hESC. In the rest of Europe, reproductive medicine regulations mainly deal with IVF and prenatal diagnosis. See Alkorta (2006) for a comprehensive account of fertility medicine policies.
5. 'Egg sharing' schemes for treatment were authorised in 1998 and 'altruistic egg donation' for cloning in 2006–2007 (Plows 2010).

6. FINRRAGE was a network of women who organised the Women's Emergency Conference on the New Reproductive Technologies in Vallinge, Sweden, in March 1989. The conference provided a first formulation of common standpoints between more than 140 women from 35 countries (a majority of them from Asia) and established the transnational character of the network. Since then, FINRRAGE has cooperated with different local or national organisations in conducting a number of national, continental and international conferences.

7. Both articles were written by Dennis Campbell, a health correspondent, and did not explicitly mention donation for research.

8. The view that ARTs is a form of exploitation of Southern women by some Western feminists has been criticised as neo-colonialist and paternalistic (Widdows 2006). Nevertheless, Heather Widdows argues that Northern feminism should condemn the practices of egg donation for stem cell research and prostitution, which she views as exploitation of women.

9. Three years later, in Germany the Stem Cell Act in 2002 legalised embryonic stem cell research and the import of embryonic stem cell lines. In the UK in 2001 the HFEA Research Purposes Regulations 2001/188 permitted stem cell research, including cell nuclear replacement ('therapeutic cloning'). At the same time, the Human Reproductive Cloning Act made human reproductive cloning illegal.

10. The network was present in the USA, at the 2004 conference 'Gender and Justice in the Gene Age: A Feminist Meeting on New Reproductive and Genetic Technologies', in New York. This brought together the Center for Genetics and Society, the Committee on Women, Population and the Environment, and Our Bodies Ourselves, aiming to respond to biotechnologies from critical feminist and global social justice perspectives. In 2005 they participated at the 'Femme Globale-Gender Perspectives in the twenty-first century International Congress', at Humboldt University, Berlin.

11. Charis Thompson (2005), writing for the US context and focusing on infertility from an STS tradition, has provided a rich overview of STS scholarship and feminist scholarship of reproduction and ART. The difference between the two trends for Thompson is that STS studies 'up', relatively high-status scientists and knowledge production, whereas feminist scholarship of reproduction focuses on women as users of technologies, and is concerned with their practices of resistance and agency.

12. COREthics is associated with the Center for Bioethics & Human Dignity (CBHD), a Christian bioethics research centre of Trinity International University.

13. The Quantified Self (QS) is a community of people who use wearable devices in order to log personal information and improve various aspects

of personal life, such as mood, physical and mental performance, or other aspects of everyday life, such as air quality.

BIBLIOGRAPHY

Alkorta, I. (2006). Women's rights in European fertility medicine regulation. In H. Widdows, I. Alkorta Idiakez, & A. Emaldi Cirión (Eds.), *Women's reproductive rights*. New York: Palgrave Macmillan.

Almeling, R. (2007). Selling genes, selling gender: Egg agencies, sperm banks, and the medical market in genetic material. *American Sociology Review, 72*, 319–340.

Barad, K. M. (2007). *Meeting the universe halfway: Quantum physics and the entanglement of matter and meaning*. Durham, NC: Duke University Press.

Beck, U. (1992). *Risk society: Towards a new modernity*. London: Sage Publications.

Beeson, D., & Lippman, A. (2006). Egg harvesting for stem cell research: Medical risks and ethical problems. *Reproductive Biomedicine Online, 13*, 573–579.

Braidotti, R. (1994). *Nomadic subjects: Embodiment and sexual difference in contemporary feminist theory*. New York: Columbia University Press.

Braidotti, R. (2002). *Metamorphoses: Towards a materialist theory of becoming*. Cambridge, UK: Polity Press in association with Blackwell Publishers.

Braidotti, R. (2006). *Transpositions: On nomadic ethics*. Cambridge, UK: Polity Press.

Butler, J. (1993). *Bodies that matter*. London: Routledge.

Butler, J. (2004). *Precarious life: The powers of mourning and violence*. London: Verso.

Cooper, M. (2008). *Life as surplus: Biotechnology and capitalism in the neoliberal era*. Washington: University of Washington Press.

Corea, G. (1985). *The mother machine: Reproductive technologies from artificial insemination to artificial wombs*. New York: Harper and Row.

Corner House (2005). Responses to the consultation on the Review of the Human Fertilisation and Embryology Act, 2006, Department of Health, The National Archives. http://collections.europarchive.org/tna/20100509080731/ http://dh.gov.uk/en/Consultations/Responsestoconsultations/DH_4132777. Accessed 19 August 2010.

Crowe, C. (1985). Women want it: In vitro fertilisation and women's motivations for participation. *Women's Studies International Forum, 8*, 547–552.

Dean, J. (2009). *Democracy and other neoliberal fantasies: Communicative capitalism and left politics*. Durham, NC: Duke University Press.

Dean, J. (2010). Affective networks. *MediaTropes, 2*(2), 19–44.

Dickenson, D. (2001). *Ethical issues in maternal-fetal medicine*. Cambridge: Cambridge University Press.

Dickenson, D. (2006). The lady vanishes: What's missing from the stem cell debate. *Journal of Bioethical Inquiry, 3,* 43–54.

Dickenson, D. (2007). *Property in the body: Feminist perspectives.* Cambridge: Cambridge University Press.

Epstein, S. (1995). The construction of lay expertise: AIDS activism and the forging of credibility in the reform of clinical trials. *Science, Technology, and Human Values, 20,* 408–437.

Epstein, S. (1996). *Impure science: AIDS, activism, and the politics of knowledge.* Berkeley: University of California Press.

Epstein, S. (2000). Democracy, expertise, and AIDS treatment activism. In D. L. Kleinman (Ed.), *Science, technology, and democracy.* Albany: State University of New York Press.

Evans, D. G. R., Barwell, J., Eccles, D. M., Collins, A., Izatt, L., Jacobs, C., Donaldson, A., Brady, A. F., Cuthbert, A., Harrison, R., & Thomas, S. (2014). The Angelina Jolie effect: How high celebrity profile can have a major impact on provision of cancer related services. *Breast Cancer Research, 16*(5), 1.

Fotopoulou, A. (2014). The quantified self community, lifelogging and the making of 'smart' publics. *Open Democracy, Participation Now.* 10 September 2014. http://www.opendemocracy.net/participation-now/aristea-fotopou lou/quantified-self-community-lifelogging-and-making-of-'smart'-pub Accessed 22 February 2015.

Fotopoulou, A., & O'riordan, K. (2016). Training to self-care: Fitness tracking, biopedagogy and the healthy consumer. *Health Sociology Review, 25,* 3.

Foucault, M. (1978). *The history of sexuality. Vol. 1: The will to knowledge.* London: Penguin Books Ltd.

Foucault, M. (2008). *The birth of biopolitics: Lectures at the Collège de France, 1978–79.* Basingstoke: Palgrave Macmillan.

Fox Keller, E. (1995). *Reflections on gender and science.* New Haven and London: Yale University Press.

Franklin, S. (2007). 'Crook' Pipettes: Embryonic emigrations from agriculture to reproductive biomedicine. *Studies in History and Philosophy of Science Part C: Studies in History and Philosophy of Biological and Biomedical Sciences, 38,* 358–373.

Franklin, S., & Lock, M. M. (2003). *Remaking life & death: Toward an anthropology of the biosciences.* Santa Fe: School of American Research Press.

Gallagher, J. (2011). Lisa Jardine starts egg donor compensation discussion, *BBC News,* 17 January. http://www.bbc.co.uk/news/health-12193598. Accessed 19 April 2011.

Gill, R. (2007). *Gender and the media.* Cambridge, UK: Polity Press.

Gunnarsdottir, K., Dijk, N. V., Fotopoulou, A., Guimarães Pereira, Â., O'riordan, K., Rommetveit, K., & Vesnic-Alujevic, L. 2015. Gadgets on the move and in stasis: Consumer and medical electronics, what's the difference? (summary of findings and policy recommendations).

Haran, J., et al. (2008). *Human cloning in the media: From science fiction to science practice*. London: Routledge.

Haraway, D. (1988). Situated knowledges: The science question in feminism and the privilege of partial perspective. *Feminist Studies, 14*, 575–599.

Haraway, D. J. (1997). *ModestWitness@secondMillennium. FemaleManMeets-OncoMouse: Feminism and technoscience*. New York: Routledge.

Harding, S. G. (1991). *Whose science? Whose knowledge?: Thinking from women's lives*. New York: Cornell University Press.

Hardt, M., & Negri, A. (2000). *Empire*. Cambridge, MA: Harvard University Press.

Hardt, M., & Negri, A. (2005). *Multitude: War and democracy in the age of empire*. New York: Penguin.

HFEA (2010). Donation review. http://www.hfea.gov.uk/5605.html. Accessed 19 August 2010.

HFEA (2011). HFEA general directions given under the Human Fertilisation and Embryology Act 1990 as amended. Gamete and embryo donation. http://www.hfea.gov.uk/docs/2009-06-03_GENERAL_DIRECTIONS_0001_Gamete_and_Embryo_donation_-_approved.pdf. Accessed 19 August 2011.

Laclau, E. (2004). Glimpsing the future. In S. Critchley & O. Marchart (Eds.), *Laclau: A critical reader* (pp. 279–328). London: Routledge.

Latour, B., & Weibel, P. (2005). *Making things public: Atmospheres of democracy*. Karlsruhe, Germany, ZKM/Center for Art and Media in Karlsruhe. Cambridge, MA: MIT Press.

Lazzarato, M. (1996). Immaterial labour. In S. Makdidi, C. Casarino, & R. Karl (Eds.), *Marxism beyond Marxism*. London: Routledge.

Lazzarato, M. (2009). Neoliberalism in Action. *Theory, Culture & Society, 26*, 109–133.

Longhurst, R. (2009). YouTube: A new space for birth?. *Feminist Review, 93*, 46–63.

Lupton, D. (2015). Quantified sex: A critical analysis of sexual and reproductive self-tracking using apps. *Culture, Health & Sexuality, 17*(4), 440–453.

Marres, N. (2004). Tracing the trajectories of issues, and their democratic deficits, on the web: The case of the development gateway and its doubles. *Information Technology & People, 17*, 124–149.

Marres, N. (2006). Net-work is format work: The issue-network as a site of politics and the challenge of making info-technology part of civil society. In J. Dean, J. W. Anderson, & G. Lovink (Eds.), *Reformatting politics: Information technology and global civil society*. New York: Routledge.

Marres, N. (2007). The issues deserve more credit: Pragmatist contributions to the study of public involvement in controversy. *Social Studies of Science, 37*, 759–780.

Mcrobbie, A. (2009). *The aftermath of feminism*. London: Sage.

Merchant, C. (1980). *The death of nature: Women, ecology, and the scientific revolution*. San Francisco: Harper & Row.

Mies, M. (1986). *Patriarchy and accumulation on a world scale: Women in the international division of labour*. London: Zed Books.

Mies, M., & Shiva, V. (1993). *Ecofeminism*. Halifax: Zed Books.

Mitchell, R., & Thurtle, P. (Eds.), (2004). *Data made flesh: Embodying information*. London: Routledge.

Murdoch, A. (2009). Interview by Jane Garvey, woman's hour, BBC radio 4. [audio] 14 December 2009.

Murphy, M. (2012). *Seizing the means of reproduction: Entanglements of feminism, health, and technoscience*. Durham, NC: Duke University Press.

Nair, S., Kirbat, P., & Sexton, S. (2004). A decade after Cairo: Women's health in a free market economy. Sturminster Newton, Briefing, 31. The Corner House. http://www.thecornerhouse.org.uk/resource/decade-after-cairo. Accessed 16 August 2011.

Nih National Cancer Institute (2016). BRCA1 and BRCA2: Cancer risk and genetic testing. http://www.cancer.gov/about-cancer/causes-prevention/genetics/brca-fact-sheet

Nisker, J. (2013). A public health education initiative for women with a family history of breast/ovarian cancer: Why did it take Angelina Jolie?. *Journal of Obstetrics and Gynaecology Canada*, 35(8), 689–691.

No2Eggsploitation (2009a). Action alert: No to eggsploitation! Protect women from risks of egg donation! [blog]. 28 September. http://no2eggsploitation.wordpress.com/2009/09/28/no2eggsploitation/. Accessed 16 August 2011

No2Eggsploitation (2009b). Guest post: No to Eggsploitation! [blog] 15 October. https://no2eggsploitation.wordpress.com/2011/01/16/43/. Accessed 16 August 2011.

Noar, S. M., Althouse, B. M., Ayers, J. W., Francis, D. B., & Ribisl, K. M. (2015). Cancer information seeking in the digital age effects of Angelina Jolie's prophylactic mastectomy announcement. *Medical Decision Making*, 35(1), 16–21.

O'riordan, K., & Haran, J. (2009). From reproduction to research. *Feminist Theory*, 10, 191–210.

Pateman, C. (1988). *The sexual contract*. Stanford, CA: Stanford University Press.

Plows, A. (2008). Egg donation in the UK: Tracing emergent networks of feminist engagement in relation to HFEA policy shifts in 2006. In F. Molfino & F. Zucco (Eds.), *Women in biotechnology: Creating interfaces*. Dordrecht: Springer.

Plows, A. (2009). James Hazell show, BBC Suffolk. BBC Radio 4. 10 December. http://www.bbc.co.uk/iplayer/episode/p005f6cl/jameshazell10122009. Accessed 10 December 2009.

Plows, A. (2010). *Debating human genetics: Contemporary issues in public policy and ethics*. London: Routledge.

Rabinow, P. (1999). Artificiality and enlightenment: From sociobiology to biosociality. In M. Biagioli (Ed.), *The science studies reader*. New York: Routledge.
Rabinow, P., & Rose, N. (2006). Biopower today. *Biosocieties, 1*, 195–217.
ReproKult (2005). Position on the harvesting and marketing of egg cells, women's forum on reproductive technologies. http://www.reprokult.de/trading_egg_cells.pdf. Accessed 23 August 2009.
Rose, N. (2001). The politics of life itself. *Theory, Culture and Society, 18*, 1–30.
Sexton, S. (1999). If cloning is the answer, what was the question? Power and decision-making in the geneticisation of health. Sturminster Newton, Corner House. http://www.thecornerhouse.org.uk/resource/if-cloning-answer-what-was-question. Accessed 20 March 2010.
Sexton, S. (2005). Transforming 'waste' into 'resource': From women's eggs to economics for women. Presentation, the Corner House, at commodification and commercialisation of women's bodies in reproductive technologies – perspectives for feminist intervention, at the femme globale – Gender perspectives in the 21st century international congress, Humboldt University, Berlin. http://www.reprokult.de/sexton.pdf. Accessed 20 August 2009.
Spallone, P., & Steinberg, D. L. (1987). *Made to order: The myth of reproductive and genetic progress*. New York: Pergamon Press.
Sunder Rajan, K. (2006). *Biocapital: The constitution of postgenomic life*. Durham, NC: Duke University Press.
Terranova, T. (2004). *Network culture: Politics for the information age*. London: Pluto Press.
Thacker, E. (2004). *Biomedia*. Minneapolis: University of Minnesota Press.
Thompson, C. (2005). *Making parents: The ontological choreography of reproductive technologies*. Cambridge, MA: MIT Press.
Thornham, H. (2015). Irreconcilability in the digital: Gender, technological imaginings and maternal subjectivity. *Feminist Review, 110*(110), 1–17.
Tyler, I. (2011). Pregnant beauty: Maternal femininities under neoliberalism. In Gill, R. & Scharff, C. (Eds.), *New femininities: Postfeminism, neoliberalism, and subjectivity* (pp. 21–36). Basingstoke: Palgrave Macmillan.
Wajcman, J. (1991). *Feminism confronts technology*. University Park, PA: Pennsylvania State University Press.
Waldby, C., & Cooper, M. (2006). The biopolitics of reproduction: post-fordist biotechnology and women's clinical labour. Working paper, Global Biopolitics Research Group. http://www.kcl.ac.uk/content/1/c6/03/03/65/wp15.pdf. Accessed 17 July 2011.
Waldby, C., & Cooper, M. (2010). From reproductive work to regenerative labour: The female body and the stem cell industries. *Feminist Theory, 11*, 3–22.
Widdows, H. (2006). Introduction. In Widdows, H., Alkorta Idiakez, I., & Emaldi Cirión, A. (Eds.), *Women's reproductive rights*. Basingstoke: Palgrave Macmillan.

CHAPTER 5

Space, Locality and Connectivity: The End of Identity Politics as We Know It?

The key claim of this book is that doing feminist and queer politics involves enacting ourselves as activists, embodied and political subjects through media practices, technologies and their imaginaries. In this chapter, I am driven by the need to understand what digital networking technologies mean for queer activists, and how their sense of belonging and politics is shaped in the digital era. Queer youth, like indeed all youth today, use social media networks to socialise, to inhabit a space of belonging, to share intimate stories and to find information about LGBT issues (Crowley 2010; De Ridder 2015; Jenzen and Karl 2014; Pullen 2014). Homophobic cyber-bullying and trolling, however, alert us to a darker aspect of dense connectivity. The many cases of gay teen suicides, often directly linked to online hate speech and homophobic bullying, signpost how fundamentally social media have changed our lives, and how our lives are more visibly interconnected than ever before in digital networks. The concentrated queer cultural self-production that follows dark events such as gay or trans suicides usually employs the same media as the abusers – social media platforms like YouTube, Tumblr, Twitter and Facebook. The campaign 'It Gets Better' for instance, initiated by American media figure Dan Savage, is a key moment where queer digital media production and activist consciousness converged. This is not the only campaign that relied heavily on sharing visual material in social media platforms. Today, most LGBT activist campaigns do, and indeed this should come as no surprise; as Tiidenberg and

© The Author(s) 2016   123
A. Fotopoulou, *Feminist Activism and Digital Networks*,
Palgrave Studies in Communication for Social Change,
DOI 10.1057/978-1-137-50471-5_5

Gomez-Cruz note, today 'an increasing amount of communication happens through images' (2015: 77), especially on Facebook. We have seen multiple moments of queer solidarity on social media expressed in visual terms. The Facebook translucent rainbow flag filter, for example, was available to users just after the Supreme Court deemed same-sex marriage legal across the USA in June 2015. With 26 million active rainbow coloured profiles within only the first few days of the campaign, the argument that queer rights and life is under-represented in mainstream media (Pullen 2014) may not be entirely accurate. But do these kinds of campaigns, and their endorsement by mainstream heterosexual culture, mean that LGBT activism and identity politics are mainly performed online? Is social media where we should be looking when we attempt to understand queer activism, community and intimacy today? And if community has really migrated online, what happens to the social, the intimate and the embodied?

In what follows, I offer a substantial account of how locality, sociality and LGBT history all play a key role in the formation of political identity for queer activist cultures. Drawing from ethnographic analysis of an anarcho-queer, DIY[1] and transient gender/queer activist group in Brighton, Queer Mutiny (QM), I argue that, for queer political cultures, there is much more at stake than using social media. Social networking is an important component of cultural production and contributes to identity formation, especially because it is a means of documenting and promoting assets of community life. But as my study shows, queer communities and cultural activism are woven in the shadow play of embodied affective relations on the ground. They are shaped by pedagogical workshops, where peer support and learning are central. And they are articulated during lengthy workshops in queer feminist autonomous spaces. By tracing how, through their asynchronous media practices, QM activists built a strong sense of place, and maintained an active link between the past, the present and the future, my discussion delineates how digital technologies today offer both tensions and opportunities to queer political projects.

A Sense of Place

My exploration concentrates on a particular locality: Brighton, a city located geographically in the South East of the UK. But places and communities are not static and waiting to be researched or written about. A place is a particular articulated moment of intersecting, dynamic social relations (Massey 1994: 5). Our physical experiences, our memories and social interactions, including those happening in social media networks, all inform our sense of place. Brighton is certainly a result of its histories, including its strong LGBT activist history, and the interactions of its transient and fluctuating population of visitors and inhabitants. The local connections of queer political constellations in the area, and the more contemporary global connections through digital media, enable a distinct form of cultural activism, which is my focus here. My argument is based on the premise that the production of space and the formation of community have been central projects for identity politics; think, for example the activism of ACT UP, Pride marches, kiss-ins and unisex toilets (Bell and Valentine 1995; Browne et al. 2007; Duncan 1996; Munt 1998). These all show how claiming space is a struggle for the right to be visible and be present as a living body in everyday reality and in the world. Queer public presence is, however, increasingly and steadily being reduced to acceptable expressions of sexuality and in foreclosed consumption spaces and 'zones', both in the media and in everyday life, as critical literature has been well documented (see Duggan 2002; Rubin 1998). Facebook and other social media platforms can indeed operate as such foreclosed consumption zones, with their strict adherence to specific norms and algorithmic categorisation of relationships and behaviours. As they are 'carefully managed spaces of civility with clear commercial end aims, users are increasingly up against restricting limitations that make them seek out alternatives' (Jenzen 2016: n.p.). The question that arises thus is, in this context of foreclosure and control, demarcated on the one hand, by intense commercialisation of the LGBT scene, and on the other, by the commercial and algorithmic characteristics of digital platforms, how do contemporary queer activist cultures produce space and preserve the life of the community?

There are often significant tensions between an imagined global political community around LGBT rights and the materialisation of local queer communities. As I will explain in the second part of the chapter, queer activist cultures are performatively/materially produced through certain place-specific communicative acts, both online and offline. In my empirical case, there are two main sets of communicative practices: a counteracting and a generative. The counteractive or reactive communicative practices of the group under investigation comprise primarily of responses to the politics of Brighton Pride. But queer subjectivity in this case is also produced through communicative acts around expectations of physical mobility and online connectivity for queer people. As we will see, participants often experienced digital networks and the exposure these entail as distinctively unsafe, which resulted in ambivalence about, and sometimes, even resistance to their use. Most of this use ultimately aimed at strengthening local social bonds and community connections, and indeed developing a sense of home and permanence, which, following Morley (2001), I will suggest constitutes a media practice of reterritorialisation.

The second set of communicative acts that I focus on is generative; it is the production of memories, experiences, physical and symbolic settings for, and even models of queer life. In an article on queer counterpublics, Berlant and Warner (1998) argued that because for queer cultures there is no primary register, as is the case for heterosexual culture and its set of practices, they create this register themselves with reference to non-standard intimacies.[2] Queer counterpublics are:

> a world-making project, where 'world,' like 'public,' differs from community or group because it necessarily includes more people than can be identified, more spaces than can be mapped beyond a few reference points, modes of feeling that can be learned rather than experienced as a birth right … World making, as much in the mode of dirty talk as of print-mediated representation, is dispersed through incommensurate registers, by definition unrealizable as community or identity. (Berlant and Warner 1998: 558)

As we will see, social media and networking platforms are fundamental in this project of world-making; photographic memories, fanzines and conversations that circulated in mailing lists, weblogs, social networks and in gatherings on the ground created points of reference for the group, which were essential for imagining queer community beyond an institution, nation, property or place. These practices of exchanging stories had two important functions: they left online affective traces (Karatzogianni and Kuntsman 2012) of connecting and socialising, and they functioned as primary references of a local political community, joining the past with the future. However, what is also significant here is how the project of world-making for queer political cultures and publics was distinctly pedagogical. As mentioned in Chapter 1 with reference to Stephansen's (2016) theorisation of citizen media as practice, shifting the focus to these pedagogic aspects of activist media practices and their social significance is important because it enables us to understand the role of digital networks beyond the circulation of discourse – ideas, messages and content. Media practices that include but are not limited to digital media facilitate the formation of a coun-terpublic by making social bonds more dense and substantial, and by prioritising situated experience. Meanwhile, I note the complex and overlapping configurations of time that these practices enabled; some-times immediate and sometimes slow, sometimes looping between past, present and future, these temporalities of interaction engaged different public worlds in this project of queer world-making.

But before delving any deeper into queer world-making, one may ask, what does 'queer' mean? There is no straight answer to this question; 'queer' is a contested term, and there are different understandings of its meaning and political potential. During the 1990s, 'queer' became a distinct scholarly and political field as an alternative to lesbian and gay politics (see, e.g. Michael Warner 1993a). Max H. Kirsch (2000), for example, argued that queer constituted a lifestyle choice that accepted dominant culture and consumerism by the lesbian and gay community in order to gain higher social status (p. 73), only to transform into a niche economic force. Others, like Sharon Smith (1994), in a Marxist critique of identity politics, argued that ideas of autonomy characterised the left and the practices of anti-AIDS activism at the time. The politics of difference, that is, those of queering for Smith made it difficult to imagine and realise a unified, lasting, militant movement that could fight oppres-sion. Other genealogies of queer focused on the role that AIDS activism played in forming queer politics of alliance between lesbians and gay men. These alliances were often perceived as resulting in lesbians 'going fag'; in other words adopting attitudes and behaviours of gay men like role-playing and non-monogamy (Queen and Schimel 2001). Queer feminism in this work was presented as a 'lustful identity' (Schwartz cited in Henry 2004: 121) that opposed what was seen as a de-sexualised lesbian-feminist politics.[3] For Stevi Jackson and Sue Scott (1996), the political project of queer as expressed in kiss-ins, gender-fuck performance and 'mock wed-dings' was indeed a continuation of the critique of heterosexuality that second-wave feminism initiated. For them, queer demonstrated how gender and sexuality are products of discourse rather than given realities, and it continued from a tradition in the field of work which views female sexuality as a social construction. But more broadly, 'queer' in queer studies in the last twenty years (Davies 2005; Giffney 2004; Halberstam 2005) operates as a way of contesting, homogenising and normalising practices, whether these come from hegemonic heterosexual discourses, from mainstream LGBT politics (Seidman 1996), or from the de-sexualised spaces of academia (Warner 1993a: xxvi).

So let me, at this point, clarify what 'queer' means for me in this chapter, and in the book as a whole. It is, first, the way group participants identified with a political position. For some of them, it signified gender fluidity, for others trans-activism, and/or a call to anti-capitalist politics. Second, as I have written elsewhere (Fotopoulou 2013a), for me 'queering' is an active process of making boundaries visible and stressing their artificiality (Browne 2006) – a way 'to challenge and break apart conventional categories' (Doty cited in Giffney 2004:73). This book is itself a queer project, because it attempts to disrupt the dualism information/materiality by highlighting the production of embodied local political formations through digital network practices.

GAY PRIDE, THE 'VILLAGE' AND CONSUMERISM

In order to understand Brighton's present queer activism and its world-making, future-oriented project, let us look at how it has been informed by the past. Often called the San Francisco of Europe, Brighton reveals an important LGBT activist history, while in urban, everyday public spaces, ordinary LGBT communities are very prominent. Alongside London and Manchester, Brighton has been one of the three metropolitan areas in the UK with a considerable number of lesbian and gay spaces like saunas and bars (Casey 2004:447), but also gay and lesbian-friendly policies. For instance, the Brighton and Hove Council has actively promoted the Civil Partnership Bill proposals for legal status for same-sex couples (granted under the 2004 Civil Partnership Act),[4] has an official housing strategy that aims to establish better LGBT community safety[5] and performed the first ever same-sex marriage in the UK in 2013. A survey conducted in 2008 showed that more than half of the respondents had moved to Brighton and Hove because of the LGBT community and scene, which further illustrates how the city is widely conceived by LGBT identified people to be a gay centre ('Count Me In' 2001).[6]

Brighton saw the establishment of a strong commercial nightclub scene around the Kemptown 'village' in the 1990s, and the publication of its own free gay magazines, *GScene* and *3sixty*. Soon, however, most venues around the UK came into heterosexual and corporate ownership, attracting mainly 'hen' parties and straight men.[7] As these commercial spaces gained popularity in the 1980s, notably also amongst heterosexual women

(Skeggs 1999), they prompted significant critical work about identity, commercialisation and de-politicisation of lesbian and gay sub-cultures. For example, Alan Sinfield (1998) traced post-1980s marketing styles and noted the transitions from covert marketing strategies to explicit address to the 'pink pound'. Gay was promoted as *cool*, as multinational corporations expanded to new niche markets.

This focus on consuming leisure experience as a way of claiming lesbian and gay identity, and the concurrent opening up of lesbian and gay spaces to heterosexual consumers, has also raised issues of and comfort and safety for the LGBT population. As I write, the memory of the grim Orlando shooting is still fresh and painful, and I cannot stop thinking about how safety and visibility are still very much at stake in commercial LGBT spaces. Pride is one such commercial space, constructed around an annual, often weeklong event in many cities around the UK. Brighton Pride as a charitable organisation aims to financially support local LGBT and queer (LGBTQ) community groups, and in 2009 an entry fee to Preston Park, where the Parade terminates, was established. The LGBT community met this development with ambivalence, but as it appeared in local media and consultations at the time, Brighton Pride is seen as a carnival that needs to be economically viable, and is considered by both locals and local governance as a major annual attraction.[8] Since 2000, the LGBTQ community, commercial stakeholders (pubs, clubs and drag artists) and statutory services (the police, primary care trust and the council) have been working in collaboration to support Brighton Pride.

Along with various local businesses targeting LGBT visitors, Pride is regularly featured on the Brighton and Hove Council website, and on the official tourist website, *VisitBrighton.com*.[9] Considering that the event was at the time also rebranded from 'Gay Pride' to 'Brighton Pride', merging the event with the *city* rather than the sexual identity, it might not be an exaggeration to say that Brighton Pride is today largely a de-politicised event.

The de-politicisation of LGBT identities due to commercialisation of the scene become even more obvious if we consider how lesbian and gay activism manifested in the past. The first Brighton Gay [?] Pride March took place as early as 1991, and was introduced by the coalition Brighton Area Action against Section 28. This campaign mobilised local lesbian groups and disrupted Princess Diana's address to the International Congress for the Family in Brighton in 1990. The Brighton Lesbian Group (BLG) was active from 1976 to 1982, but radical lesbian and feminist politics continued to be strong in Brighton throughout the 1980s. There are significant achievements of this period, such as the Brighton Women's Centre, which still operates today, and the Brighton Lesbian Line. More generally, Brighton has been prominent in LGBT rights activism since the establishment of the Sussex Gay Liberation Front (SGLF)[10] at the University of Sussex in 1971.[11] It was not until 1997 that Pride became a Council-supported event and gradually attracted major sponsorship from other sources.

Today various local LGBTQ-led[12] media and Brighton-based newspapers like the *Argus* and the *Leader* operate as forum of discussion around local issues, like Brighton Pride. At the same time, community-focused research projects like *Count Me In* and *Count Me In Too, Livable Lives* and *Make, Share, Care*, try to influence local policy by accounting for those usually excluded from survey research, like bisexual and trans people, and engage queer youth with social media platforms.[13] Joint action that brings together universities and community-sector organisations has been a dominant mode of pursuing social change for LGBTQ people living in Brighton.[14] The LGBTQ community sector, commercial imperatives, academic projects and local governance are closely intertwined in the production of spaces in the city.

THE POLITICAL POTENTIAL OF COMMODIFICATION

As we will see, in its early formation Queer Mutiny (from here on QM) raised decisive questions about commodification and Brighton's LGBT scene. Given the long history of LGBT activism and community action in the city, and the growing links between the community and the academy, such questions are increasingly complicated and digital media are integral to this. But linking commodification and de-politicisation may not be as straightforward as it seems; is it all just about 'selling out'? First of all, we need to consider that understandings of commodification and de-politicisation of LGBTQ cultures result from the assumption that consumer publics are passive. But consumers of Pride have in some cases been thought to be politically motivated and to in fact resist dominant ideologies (Kates and Belk 2001). In an ethnographic study of five Pride events, Kates and Belk (2001) interpreted the experience as a 'multi-layered form of consumption-related cultural resistance' (p 393) Berlant and Freeman (1992) also reflect, in relation to Queer Nation tactics, that consumer pleasure is central to the transformation of public culture. Yet does this everyday consumer resistance actually change social relations of subordination? What does it mean, for example, for exclusions on the basis of race, ethnicity, class and gender (and intersections thereof)?

Bell and Binnie (2004) and Binnie (2010) offer fundamental insight in addressing these questions. They argued that the incorporation of 'gay villages' and commodified gay spaces into the agendas of local urban governance is a symptom of neoliberal ideologies. This work echoes Duggan's (2002) claims of a 'new homonormativity', a tendency in North American LGBTQ politics to 'purify' progressive and radical democratic politics. Duggan suggested that diversity claims for sexual dissidence have transformed into claims for recognition of a 'domesticated, depoliticised privacy' (2002: 190). The article was highly critical of LGBTQ politics conforming to the cultural politics of neoliberalism, which Duggan understood as outcomes of the 'third way' rhetoric of the early 1990s.[15] In *Authenticating queer spaces*, Bell and Binnie expressed similar fears for the mainstreaming of LGBTQ politics, and placed sexual citizenship at the heart of urban entrepreneurialism (2004: 1807). More recently, Binnie (2010) emphasised the ambivalent relationship between non-normative sexualities and neoliberalism. He suggested that an ethical and political consumption and tourism is possible, and it can even be understood as solidarity activism. In these respects, Pride can be understood as a commodified sexualised space, produced through urban governance in Brighton and Hove – and moreover as an event that stands for a broader policy in Brighton.

This brief historical account of how Brighton developed commercially around Pride, alongside the different approaches to 'queer' that I outlined earlier, raise some necessary questions about the state of queer activism today within a wider politics of resistance. Do queer activism and its cultures have a voice within Leftist politics for example? And how do local LGBT politics, in particular, counter or welcome the global tendencies of homogenisation that are so inextricably linked to digital media technologies? In the next part of this chapter, I analyse how queer political identities form in this context. As we will see, belonging, transformation and making 'safe' spaces were key themes in the narration of Brighton queer activists.

QUEER MUTINY BRIGHTON AS A COUNTERPUBLIC: QUEER MUTINY AND ANTI-CAPITALIST POLITICS

I will now move to look closely at the communicative tactics of QM, and their understandings of space and activism as these emerged from my ethnographic study. QM is a DIY, anarcho-queer organisation, with branches in Edinburgh, London, Brighton, Bristol, Cardiff and Leeds in the UK. I chose to study the Brighton group at an early stage of research for this book in 2009, when I imagined my project to be to a celebratory approach to DIY cultural politics[16] and everyday queer resistance. At the time, QM was attempting to form again after a long pause, and it was accessible to me since members of the group also had links to the academic community where I belonged. I also felt sympathetic to the anti-consumerist leftist attitudes of the group. During my fieldwork, I attended meetings with the intention to observe general attitudes to communication technologies and sharing of information online.[17] I was interested in gaining insight about what 'activism' meant for participants, and how they perceived ideas of community online and offline.[18]

My ethnographic research was guided by a number of questions. I was primarily motivated by the need to understand how the concepts of community and connectivity were changing for Brighton queer communities. But I also found it important to examine how the meaning and practices of space and place were changing with connectivity and mobile technologies. What did it mean for queer activism and culture that space and community are changing with digital media technologies? I tried to understand how the history of Brighton activism, Brighton Pride and the commercialisation of the scene shaped the political voice and activist practices of QM.

The people I interviewed also organised Brighton West Hill Wotever, a spin off night for Club Wotever and Wotever World,[19] which took place at the community space Westhill Community Hall. They had, from May 2007 to March 2009, organised six events, mainly of music and drag king performances and several workshops about gender and sexuality. Although Brighton Wotever operated independently of the London Wotever World, it used its name and ethos. From the wider network of the three main interviewees I contacted the organisers of the parties 'Slut Disco', 'Out of the Bedroom and Into the Streets' and three people from 'BiFest Brighton 2009' Conference. These were gender bending, alternative music and dance parties that happened monthly or more sporadically at the Cowley Club, Brighton's autonomous social centre.

QM formed twice; once in 2005, and then again in 2009. The 2005 formation was a DIY community strongly attached to the ethics of anti-copyright, veganism, squatting, not-for-profit events, anti-hierarchical organisation and sharing of skills. The online forms of communication established at that time were consistent with open source culture. For example, the email list was hosted at the autonomous Seattle-based *riseup. net*[20] server, and their website was in wiki form.[21] This first configuration of the group created three zines and various cultural events like film viewings. Zines fit well with the DIY origins of the group – remember that zines have been an essential medium for the dissemination of ideas and news beyond mainstream and corporate owned communication channels prior to social media, especially in the 1990s, and also took up a large part of DIY activity in various groups (see Atton 2002). QM used the Cowley Club as a meeting space. It also supported campaigns by the wider queer community, which at the time formed around Queeruption.[22] The first QM zine came out in Spring 2006 and had a 'Fuck authority' sign on the front page (Fig. 5.1). On the first page of the QM Brighton Zine (2006: 1) the group stated:

> Queer Mutiny is a random group of radical queer activists who get together to: Meet each other. Share ideas. Work together. Challenge norms of gender and sexuality. Plan/organise actions and campaigns. Create a safe space for likeminded people to gather.

From the polemic attitude of the zine, it is evident that Gay Shame and Queer Nation, key queer activist groups in the USA, served as inspiration for QM. Queer Nation,[23] in particular, shifted the meaning of 'safe' nation from that of juridical safety (from discrimination) to that of safety to demonstrate and be visible in national publics (Berlant and Freeman 1992). Queer Nation incorporated consumerism strategically in their tactics; they invaded spaces which they thought to be heteronormative but apolitical, for example, by doing kiss-ins in shopping malls. Though QM concurred with Queer Nation's non-assimilationist politics[24] and was involved in a direct action, as I discuss later, generally they did not adopt such tactics. For example, in a Queer Mutiny Brighton (2006: 1) it was stated: 'Against consumerism, assimilation, representation and the rest of shit that claims to be the "gay lifestyle"'. Nonetheless, for QM the

mutineer (ˌmjuːtɪˈnɪə) *n*. a person who mutinies.

Fig. 5.1   The front cover of the first QM Zine

target of opposition was primarily Brighton's LGBT mainstream culture, rather than a national LGBT agenda.

One of the most aggressive communicative schemes that contributed to building a distinct counter identity for the group was the pornographic photo session entitled 'Black Bloc Porn', featuring the group members holding machine guns and wearing masks.[25] This depiction was arguably inconsistent with the group's anti-war position, as this had been previously communicated in a divisive intervention at the 2005 Pride. Then, QM had invaded the march and disrupted the recruitment stalls of the British Army and Navy. According to one of my informants, the action was not the result of consensual decision-making and caused tension within the group.

QM in this first zine that stated, 'Brighton is a transient village' (2006: 3), where wealthy gay people spend money and move away. As queer mutineers, they aimed to object to LGBT privileges and create a local queer community that was prepared to contest gay unity – as it would be the case with the inclusion of the military stalls, for instance – in favour of political intervention. 'Queer' was a political position intimately connected to anti-capitalist politics for the group, and in the next issues the discourse gradually shifted from building a community, to creating safe spaces of their own (rather than assuming that the city is a 'safe space'), to building a movement and getting ready for *the revolution*. As the first page of the third and last zine of the first QM formation (subtitled 'Slave to the Revolution') indicated, this movement would be a queer, anti-authoritarian, and anti-capitalist.[26] The group also drew links to non-local happenings, like the Argentinian queer-anarchist squats, and increasingly became less Brighton-focused. This development coincided with several members moving away from Brighton. Subsequently, only few of the people who initiated the reunion of January 2009 were associated with this older group. Nonetheless, the queer anti-capitalist identity of QM remained a counter response to the commodification of the local lesbian and gay subculture (see Fig. 5.2). As the 2009 Queer Mutiny Manifesto (2009: 1) stated:

> We experience feeling marginalised and fetishized within LGBT spaces, within which we are 'supposed' to feel safe. We give two fingers up to happy clappy gay culture. We want to participate in and ourselves create DIY independent culture.

Queer Mutiny is a loose bunch of queers of all sexualities who meet regularly in Brighton to talk to each other, socialise and get active. We are the sum of parts, not just one box to tick. We are a collective. We have differing opinions, yet we are united in fighting for a queer understanding of gender and sexuality, DIY and not-for-profit culture. If you agree or disagree with anything you read, please contact us via email, queermutinybrighton@lists.riseup.net and/or come along to one of our meetings.

QUEER MUTINY Brighton

Volume 4 Issue One
February 2009

D.I.Y, a call to Arms!

Brighton can sometimes seem a bit shit, right? How often have you sat there thinking "why's there no clubs that play my kind of music?" or "why are all the free publications (with a few mutinous exceptions) so un-inspired?" or even "why's no one projecting films onto blank walls round here?" Well, you know how to change it, right? Do It Yourself! Or with a group of like-minded friends. Or with who-ever. When you get down to it, it's a lot easier than you think! Take this zine for instance. A friend of mine had been talking about making one for ages, and Queer Mutiny as a group thought it'd be good to have some alternative, free literature around the place, and so, before we knew it, our zine was born! Everyone from the group is welcome to write for it, so if someone has something interesting they just have to get out there, they have the option to do so. We can raise issues and get them out into the public world as they arise too, publishing monthly as we do! DIY culture is important. It gives voices and expression to those who would otherwise be silent, and it is only limited by you own imaginations. Where there is a will, there is always a way. And, due to its very nature, encourages boundless creativity! So don't just sit there complaining, get out and do something about it. Write! Paint! Film! Record!

T.

Fig. 5.2   The 2009 issue of the QM Zine

QUEER METACULTURE AND QUEER CONSUMER CITIZENSHIP

'I'm not the kind of person who would put on my hood and fight the police...' Understandings of Activism

What did activism mean for those who participated in QM? During interviews, participants emphasised the differences between the 2009 QM formation and the one that took shape in 2005. Respondents had a common perception about what 'real' politics was about; this was highlighted with reference to the various expressions of anti-capitalist activism around the world. Older members, in particular, understood political action to have breadth beyond local issues and to be part of a wider activist culture, such as environmental and peace activism, No Border actions, Reclaim the Streets,[27] with direct action such as squatting and sabotaging still being important for queer politics.

Francis narrated zir participation in the first Queeruption in London in 1998.[28] Growing up in the 1990s and moving to Brighton in 1999, Francis lived through the echo of the squatters' movement.[29] When ze arrived in Brighton, Francis felt that activism with a queer orientation was absent in the town. Francis also differentiated between direct action activism, which ze thought of as confrontational, and other forms of activism that operate in a supportive way. 'That was just people meeting up and making things. So it was quite different to what we were doing, a bit more hard-core, a bit more fluffy'. Other participants understood activism as something that happens in the 'real world', while their group performed a form of 'soft activism'. In their narrations, they focused on *doing* as a key aspect of activism: confrontation on the streets and protest was the 'real' politics, rather than discussing texts and ideas indoors. Christian, for example, stated 'I'm not the kind of person who would put on my hood and fight the police... even though I want to maybe... sometimes I think that holding back and not putting yourself out and making a difference in the real world, I think I'd rather sit around and discuss things than I have that feeling that this is more valuable for me'.

This hierarchy of modes of activism that came out of participants' accounts indicated a public/private division, where wider political issues and international actions constituted *the public*, political world. According to this schema, their own actions and events were situated locally, almost privately, outside the space of 'real' political struggle. Despite this perception, in meetings QM actually discussed the US Proposition 8,[30] and California's 2008 ballot proposition that restricted same-sex marriage.

QM also took part in a G20 protest; discussed an online petition against the Oxfordshire Primary Care Trust, which obstructed NHS funding for genital reassignment surgery; and considered supporting Sussex University LGBT Society around the campaign to remove limitations on blood donation by gay men. Yet, if we were to create an imaginary grid of political identities, the construction of binaries like public/private, local/cosmopolitan, and soft/real gives a sense of how QM members perceived their own position. The group performed a counterpublic by responding to the local LGBT lifeworld with their versions of personal empowerment and queer cosmopolitan activism. This mode of engagement was full of conflicting attitudes, namely the idealisation of international queer activism and the concurrent defensiveness of Brighton. Nevertheless, as I analyse next, these same series of material and discursive, media and everyday practices produced what Berlant and Warner called a 'referential metaculture' (1998: 198).

As is the case with many queer bloggers and activists online, social networking platforms are used more to create a representational space for their community and a space of empowerment, than to create dialogue with other wider parts of civil society. In Pullen's (2014) edited volume on media cultures and queer youth, many writers consider the performative aspects of social media, even in the context of gay teenage suicides, and discuss how powerful affective performances are, including online coming-out videos. These are particularly important because they construct and indeed plant positive representations in the midst of all the negativity – including news media representation of queer youth as inherently vulnerable and in need of protectionist legislation. However, this visibility is not uncomplicated, even for queer activists. As Lenore Bell (2013) explains, Tumblr has become a unique platform to express and negotiate identity for queer social justice bloggers. Trigger warning tags are used extensively to maintain this network a 'safe space', but the use of nude self-pictures proves as a renegotiation of both safety and trans identity. Meanwhile, YouTube trans vlogs and their closeness to real-life experiences indicate the political and transformative potential of digital technology of self-representation to an even larger extent (Raun 2016). So although there is a tendency to generalise and understand social media as one uniform mode of engagement, their affordances in fact vary substantially, which subsequently encourages different forms of activist communication and action.

QM mainly used social networking platforms for the announcement of news and events, but they also used Facebook for documenting the events they organised, and for bonding as a community. During my research, Brighton's radical leftist activists were using a combination of independent media, like *riseup.net*, and commercial social networking platforms. QM used Facebook extensively in order to promote events to more 'mainstream' people in spaces of radical politics, such as the Cowley. Oddly, using a corporate platform such as Facebook was not perceived as selling out. Instead, it was heralded as a necessary marketing strategy that keeps activist ties solid. As Drew noted:

> Well, activism. Ahmm...I think Facebook is the most important thing to talk about...In terms of kind of activism, it means that I know that person is interested in that particular type...of political ideas and sexualities.... And I don't really do it to promote or anything, I do it 'cause I would like to know!

And although my respondents identified the limitations of mailing lists, they didn't seem to think that Facebook might be exclusionary. Because of the ubiquity and rising affordability of mobile phones, and eventually smartphones, Facebook is something that everyone could participate in.

Creating References: The Pedagogical Aspects of Queer World-Making

Despite their involvement in platforms that encourage two-way communication (mailing lists, mobile texting, Facebook pages and groups, wiki), QM activists used these media as mainly new channels for making announcements and for gaining visibility, rather than invitations for involvement in dialogue. In fact, they used them to differentiate from the wider LGBT community in the city, and stabilise their public common identity as a distinct queer culture. These key performative acts included posting Facebook status updates after events, updates that were consequently populated with upbeat and constructive comments about how wonderful and successful the party had been. Members uploaded photographs and 'tagged' one another on Facebook. These practices enabled a sense of belonging. As one of the organisers stressed:

> I think the Internet has been used for that, there was no queer community and now there is, we've created that, we brought all these people together and they've become friends or lovers or whatever, it's created a community, and you've got community you're more able to create more things because I

think you have that trust. And so I really think that the Internet has helped because that's how we advertise a lot of the time. (Francis 2009)

But online platforms felt too public, and therefore potentially risky for debate and personal narrative to my participants. Other research has also shown how mainstream social networking platforms are distrusted by trans youth today and how digital media continue producing negative representations and marginalisation of queer people (Jenzen 2016; Mcinroy and Craig 2015; Trans Media Watch 2010). In this context, it comes as no surprise that Christian expressed resistance to digital media platforms. Not even email lists were thought to be designated platforms of dialogue or 'virtual' versions of their communities. In one of our discussions, Christian rather thought that these forms of communication belonged in what ze named 'textual disembodied cyberworld'. The distinction between physical world as embodied and information as disembodied reminds us of the dualism that Hayles (1999) identified as the basis of 'virtuality' in the 20th century. Hayles (1999) noted how, according to this generalised understanding (and epistemic shift), meaning does not lie within the system of dissemination. Indeed, for Christian and other research participants, digital media technologies could not replace physical interactions and encounters. This is why their world-making project, although performatively remediated on social media after an event had taken place, principally took place on the ground, in the temporality of the slow, long-lasting, and even sometimes mundane organisational meetings and discussions.

In the previous chapters, I have argued that feminist and queer publics are often ambivalent about the destabilising effects of digital communicative capitalism in neoliberal times. In the last chapter, we saw, for example, how what used to be understood as the individual has come to be understood as the constantly visible body in social media environments and the malleable, extendable body in the age of apps and biosensors. I argued that these disruptions are important tenets that guide feminist responses to porn today, and that feminist subjectivity is enacted through the inherent contradictions of empowerment and vulnerability that characterise technoscientific acceleration today. When it comes to Brighton queer cultures, the generalised uncertainty about social norms and relationships in the context of commodification and increased visibility took a more specific form: it revolved around the notions of *safety, home and community*. As I illustrate next, instead of embracing the potential for physical mobility and global connectivity, queer activists used both online media and offline practices to produce a strong sense of a *locality*, in a process of 'reterritorialisation' (Morley 2001).

In his early work on belonging, David Morley (2001) developed the notion of 'reterritorialisation' as a result of his scepticism about the destabilising effects of globalisation. With a materialist focus on physical movement, he sought to address both patterns of mobility and patterns of settlement. Processes of physical and communicative deterritorialisation for Morley have been happening alongside 'reterritorialisation' processes, whereby boundaries are being reconstituted. These boundaries can address the need to regulate, for example, home use of technologies, and may signify a return to traditional forms of place-based identity. Other media and cultural studies writers aiming to understand cultural processes, like the complex connectivity that results from mobile media use, have focused on globalisation, networks and connectivity.[31] This framing is useful in the current examination of QM's digital media and cultural practices because it helps us understand how through these practices participants negotiated home and belonging, while enacting political subjectivity.

The tension between reterritorialisation and deterritorialisation in the case of QM and Westhill Wotever can be more fully understood if we recognise the queer dimensions of mobility and settlement in Brighton. Mobility has historically been a significant practice for LGBTQ people, not only as the ultimate action of leaving a homophobic environment behind, but also as an action of resistance – that of claiming space within such environments. Lesbian mobility, as this manifests in various subcultures, 'continually stamps new ground with a symbol of ownership' (Munt 1998: 120). But as Jasbir Puar writes (2002), consumption power expressed particularly through practices of tourism, political travel and mobility has been often conflated with queer liberation. 'What signals as transgressive is not just the right to sexual expression but the right to mobility through that sexual expression' (Puar 2002: 111). Nonetheless, for the participants of the study Brighton has mostly been thought to be their final destination. For example, Francis said that ze always wanted to live in Brighton. Christian talked about the sense of being in the middle of the gay scene and feeling relieved, in the sense that ze could take zer time to stabilise zer lesbian identity. Another participant told me how Brighton is a 'liberal, charming place' in contrast to the working class area ze grew up in. In most narratives of my study, queer identity was decisively determined by mobility to reach Brighton and less by a queer cosmopolitan attitude that takes the right to mobility for granted.

Thus while QM participants used social media, their practices attempted to re-organise safe local communities with clear boundaries and a predominately place-based identity. But these practices also had a temporal character. Scholars have noted how photographic archives in digital media platforms, such as Flickr, Facebook and Twitter, remediate the personal and the historical (see Mac Bean 2016; Vivienne and Burgess 2013). Digital photographic archives of queer events can be a manifestation of how queer cultures want to *feel* the past, to connect with a historical past (Mac Bean 2016). In the case of Brighton QM, it is the anxiety caused by intense mobility that makes the community, and the archive as proof of the community, essential. The group did not just remediate pleasure, intimacy and the personal in digital photographic archives to create the 'I', the personal within an undeniably glamorous crowd; their practices aimed to establish a strong community, and this performance left more than affective traces. It created primary references of a political culture, in what seemed like a future-oriented (rather than past-looking) project. In the previous chapter, I discussed Edelman's queer negativity and anti-futurism, and its contradictory influence on postporn user-generated content. There, the affective labour devoted to generating online content, as well as to connecting and participating in meetups, is thematically aimed to counter heteronormative relations and ways of living, but its form of conduct is in fact affirmative and productive. In the case of QM and other cultural activist groups, their conscious awareness of subordination and marginal status in relation to both mainstream LGBT culture and more dominant forms of activism and community action in Brighton made it necessary to create such references to an alternative queer culture and identity. So although the Facebook photographs of Brighton and London parties and events (and the way these parties were prepared and organised) are partly what Cvetkowich calls 'archives of feelings' (2003: 7), their strategic appeal to a community and their well-defined aim to manufacture a historical object outshines their character as plainly repositories of feelings. Let us see the other important aspects that this strategic claim involved: pedagogy and cultural capital.

The parties and workshops organised by QM and Westhill Wotever attempted to produce a world of safe connections and possibilities for intimacy in a plethora of imaginative ways. As organisers, these same people were resourceful and inspired in creating 'a space of entrances, exits, unsystematised lines of acquaintance, projected horizons, typifying examples, alternate routes, blockages, incommensurate geographies' (Berlant and Warner 1998: 558). Brighton as the reference point for almost the entire activity of the group made this culture meaningful. Their events were attended by a diverse group, for example young students, older people, professionals and people who were more generally engaged in the social life of the Cowley Club, as well as homeless people and people who mistook the venue for a dance club. Apart from the absence of a clear structure or accuracy in timing, at these events there was an implicit dress code for eccentricity and there were almost always homemade cakes being sold for a nominal price. The organisers thought their parties were eccentric, and, in a way, created their own opportunities for cultural capital investment and production. As one of the organisers commented: 'We are a little elitist with our music policy, but we have to be a bit strict to prevent it becoming another mediocre "gay alternative disco" of the kind churned out by Ghetto'.[32]

But the world-making project of Brighton's queer activists entailed educating those involved in the events they organised. They wished to create knowledges and spaces (both physical and spaces to think) that didn't previously exist. The QM Manifesto in February 2009 proposed:

How do we want to do it? We will educate people that there is more than the binary between heterosexual and homosexual, male and female. We will educate people so they understand queer is not just a sexuality, but a way we live our lives.

Participant narratives also stressed the pedagogic and political aspects of gatherings and how these served as a means to social change. As Francis suggested: 'it's great if people come from the more mainstream and learning about politics and zines and queer...It is like educating people, it sounds a bit evangelistic but I suppose I do feel quite evangelistic about it, I feel that's the way that the world's going to change, by educating people'. Another participant talked about making people aware of relating differently to one another.

But this emphasis on education meant that cultural capital hierarchies operated subtly within this culture.[33] The events brought together very different class identities because they could be framed as just entertainment without a political component, or as entertainment with a queer studies component. This is because there is an assumption that in order to participate in queer activism you have to have certain theoretical knowledge, which results in pressure and exclusion for people who cannot tackle the inaccessibility of queer studies texts, as Christian explained. Cultural capital also manifested in some of the members' focus on fashion. For example, in regards to the Zinefest Christian said:

> I'm really attracted to that visibly political look, it's really stereotyped – have a little bit of red, have a little bit of non-reds, look a little bit unwashed and then you're an activist – and I'm completely aware of that norm, but I'm still attracted to people who are like that, because it is a bit like, in a very personal kind of way, you're wearing your politics kind of visibly.

Thus we can see how QM's project had a solid pedagogical and political component. The practice of organising and having parties and gatherings, and using social media alongside more traditional media forms such as zines in order to disseminate information, resulted to new social relationships, to strengthening community ties and establishing collective practices and cultural capital alternative to those offered by the LGBTQ mainstream culture. These activist practices and learning spaces illustrate how QM formed as a counterpublic. Other projects that QM people initiated and run outside and beyond their group related activity using digital media exemplify the group's rich undercurrent of cultural and political activity.[34] At the same time, we may think how, through these practices, QM activists attempted to generate points of reference beyond an institution, nation, property or place. These references contributed to the production of a queer metaculture, in other words, a transient public memory for queers to use later as a common register. Participation in email lists, updating the group's webpage, sharing photographs and thoughts in social networks, as practices of exchanging stories and narrating positive experiences were central in this project. These textual traces of a queer metaculture created transient spaces of belonging and empowered the participants, despite their reservations about the usefulness or even realness of social media and digital networks. Thus while the events and discussions created a temporality of slow, everyday experience and interaction, temporalities of interaction engaged different public worlds in this project of queer world-making.

CONCLUSION

Online media have been seen to demarcate spaces of visibility, identity formation and debate, but for the activist group I examined here, these spaces were seen as less political. The political project of QM in Brighton had community building at its centre, which was achieved by a combination of pedagogic and cultural practices, which mainly involved organising and holding workshops, parties and festivals, as well as producing DIY zines and online content. Digital networks, far from being accepted as inherently empowering technologies, were resisted as activist tools. The combined practices of organising parties, safe spaces and workshops, while using social media and more traditional media forms, in order to create a community life with thick and strong ties to a place, and to a temporality, show the key role that locality, sociality and LGBT history play in the formation of political subjectivity for queer activist cultures.

Brighton has come to be widely understood as the city of transgressiveness but it largely hosts what Jasbir Puar has critically named a 'cosmopolitan queer subject' (2002) – a combination of contemporary apolitical consumerism, tourism and global NGO activism. On the one hand, intense mobility and the anxiety caused by Brighton and its queer population being increasingly transient, and on the other hand, conscious awareness of the marginal status that anarcha-queer cultures occupy in relation to mainstream LGBT culture, motivates a project of reterritorialisation in this case. As we saw, these cultures were performatively/materially produced through place-specific communicative acts, both online and offline, which reveals the tensions between how participants imagined global activism and how this activism materialised locally. Against this backdrop of neoliberalism and the 'pink pound', this chapter has shown that expressions and practices of intimacy, friendship and belonging are of key importance for local political communities.

Meanwhile, the Brighton QM group created a common online archive of photographs and messages on social networking platforms, which operates strategically as points of reference for the group by providing evidence of this strong community for the future. I have claimed that these references are essential for imagining and forming an alternative queer culture and identity in a project of queer world-making, not only because they function as affective registers, but also because they connect different and overlapping temporalities of interaction and speak to different public worlds. Stemming from situated and subjective experience of living and feeling as a queer/trans body, these implicit projects of knowledge production were consistent with feminism's historical legacy. Far, however, from conceptualising the circulation of references and discourses as the defining aspect of these queer counterpublics, I have argued that the social significance of pedagogy for QM, and the use of digital networks for stabilising social bonds helps us understand the role of digital networks as embodied, situated and social practices.

NOTES

1. DIY stands for do-it-yourself.
2. By non-standard intimacies they refer to relationships that are not necessarily linked to couples, domestic spaces, nation, property, kinship and institutional relationships.
3. Astrid Henry (2004) argued that 'queer' offered to feminism the outlaw status, the un-sanitised, non-simplistic element that the lesbian family unit and lesbian citizenship lacked.
4. The Marriage (Same Sex Couples) Act 2013 (c. 30) legalised same-sex marriage in England and Wales.
5. The strategy falls within the wider Equalities and Inclusion Policy 2008–2014 for the Council (Brighton and Hove Housing Strategy 2009).
6. The 'Count Me In' survey was carried out in 2000 and lead to a five year LGBT Community Strategy 2001–2006, actioned by Brighton & Hove City Council, the local Primary Care Trust, and other local service providers and LGBT groups. The survey continued in 'Count Me in Too' (2007–2010), a participatory action research project which identified 'marginalisation, exclusion, disenfranchisement and need amongst the LGBT in Brighton & Hove' (Browne and Lim 2008: 3). It examined 20 focus groups and 819 questionnaires. It was a joint project involving the University of Brighton and Spectrum4, supported by Brighton & Sussex Community Knowledge Exchange with funding also provided by Brighton & Hove City Primary Care Trust and Brighton & Hove City Council.
7. See Campbell (2004) about how this played out in Manchester.
8. See, for instance, the 'Gscene Editorial Comment: Where is our Pride?' by James Ledward, 26 November 2009.
9. *Visit Brighton* is one of the *Visit Britain* websites, the official sites of the British Tourist Authority. According to *Marketing Week* (Costa 2010), the gay market forms part of a strategic marketing plan for *Visit Britain*.
10. The London Gay Liberation Front (GLF) started in 1970 and by1973, GLF had effectively dissipated and had given way to its spin-off organisations. Some of these (like London Lesbian and Gay Switchboard) still thrive today. GLF followed the GLF of New York City which formed after the Stonewall riots of June 1969 – that Pride days continue to mark. In the early 1970s, American and Canadian groups and publications were in the vanguard (Hodges 2000).

11. The Brighton Ourstory Archive, established in 1989, was a source of information for my research. Brighton Ourstory is a local charitable organisation which collects material about lesbian, gay and bisexual (LGB) past, in the form of oral history interviews, exhibitions, publications, performances. It aims to increase awareness and visibility of LGB history and lives, and to establish a lesbian and gay history archive in its own premises.

12. These include *GAYBrighton.com* and *RealBrighton.com*, which are partnered web directories of event and business listings; magazines *Gscene* and *3sixty*.

13. See Olu Jenzen and Irmi Karl 'Make, Share, Care: Social Media and LGBTQ Youth Engagement', http://www.brighton.ac.uk/research/our-research/social-sciences/research-groups/transforming-sexuality-and-gender/make-share-care.aspx. Livable Lives, http://liveablelives.org.

14. One major network, of which I am also part, is the Brighton and Sussex Sexualities Network (BSSN), 'an inter-university research network aimed at supporting research and researchers who work on issues of human sexuality within the Universities of Brighton and Sussex and the wider Sussex area' (BSSN Website 2010).

15. As it appeared in Tony Blair's Labour and Bill Clinton's New Democrats, this rhetoric occupied the political mainstream and advanced politics which were 'reasonable, centrist and pragmatic' (Duggan 2002: 176).

16. DIY ethics and ideology were central in 1960s counter-culture, in punk culture in the 1970s and in the 1990s movements of green radicalism and rave culture (Mckay 1996, 1998). The Riot Grrrl movement and its zine production is also an expression of the 1990s DIY feminism (Reger 2005; Downes et al. 2007). These movements practised anti-consumerism, anti-copyright and non-hierarchical organisation.

17. Members of Queer Mutiny (QM) and Westhill Wotever agreed that the group names could be identified but all individual names have been changed. Additionally, the chapter uses gender neutral pronouns when referring to participants (See table in Appendix B, Section 5). This is out of respect for the importance of gender pronoun use for the participants, some of whom were transitioning.

18. Online, I became Facebook friends with most of the members I met at the gatherings. I accessed their network of Facebook friends and groups, their web links, their photographs and the events they attended or organised.

19. The first Wotever Club night happened in London on August 2003 and has, since then expanded to the Wotever Bar, Film Wotever, Klub Fukk, Wotever Brighton and Wotever Glasgow. The London Wotever World organised its own monthly nights at the Marlborough Theatre, in Brighton.

20. *Riseup.net* is hosted by the Riseup Collective, an autonomous Seattle-based body with worldwide members. They provide communication and computer resources to social movements and activists (Riseup Collective 2009).

21. The *Queer Mutiny Brighton Wiki* is an Open Source-based page. Its links include Facebook groups of various sub-formations like 'In Every Home...a Heartache', and Webpages of QM groups throughout the UK, Queeration London, *Indymedia* (Queer Mutiny Brighton Wiki 2009).

22. The first Queeruption gathering took place in London in 1998 and was announced as 'three days of Action, Art and Anarchy for queers of all sexualities'. It had a strong anti-consumerist agenda.

23. Queer Nation formed in 1990 in New York and mobilised against job discrimination, in the abortion rights movement and AIDS activism.

24. Notably, the Queer Mutiny Brighton zine published in Spring 2009 reproduced the 1990 Queer Nation Manifesto in its last page.

25. See Heckert and Cleminson (2011) for a collection of essays about anarchism, sexuality and ethics.

26. Similar arguments, explicitly positioned as anarchist, have appeared in Queeruption texts and other pink-black bloc texts. See Shepard 2002.

27. Reclaim the Streets is a direct action network, established in 1995, that aims to regain free access on the streets from cars and it follows the Situationist ideas about public space. Apart from parties, often called Festivals of Resistance, monthly Critical Masses are held in various cities, including Brighton.

28. The first Queeruption happened at the 121 Centre in Brixton, South London, and was announced as 'three days of Action, Art and Anarchy for queers of all sexualities'. It had a strong anti-consumerist agenda: 'We believe that there is more to being queer than what is offered to us at the moment, and want to create a radical alternative to the commercial, and a-political gay scene. The festival is open to all, and is about us all taking initiative, creating and participating, instead of just consuming a lifestyle sold to us' (Queeruption 2009).

29. The Squatters' movement launched in Britain in 1968. The movement slowly died out for a while after the south side of Villa Road was, with the squatters consent, demolished in 1977 (see Engle 2006) but was soon revived when social centres started to appear with the anti-globalisation struggle and Reclaim the Streets demonstrations.

30. California's State Constitution put the clause 'Only marriage between a man and a woman is valid or recognised in California' into effect on 5 November 2008, but did not affect existing domestic partnerships. Campaigns for and against were launched and protests occurred around the country.

31. In an earlier influential analysis, Arjun Appadurai (1995) examined territories where tourists and locals intersect, and argued that the instability of social relations in such spaces hinders the creation of 'neighbourhoods'. He thought of neighbourhoods as actual situated localities that provide the context for their subjects' production and reproduction, and render social action meaningful. Neighbourhoods in Appadurai's work produce contexts,

often in the form of 'ethnoscapes', but they also themselves constitute a set of contexts. Appadurai placed these transient communities between the local and the beyond-the-local (the 'translocal'). The production of locality is, in such spaces, an exercise of power over a hostile environment.

32. *Ghetto* is a dance club which hosts 'diverse nights for boys and girls and their straight friends', like lesbian mud wrestling (Ghetto Brighton 2009).

33. See Ward (2003) on Pride and queer cultural capital – for queers with cultural capital.

34. It is worth here making special mention of a side-project by two activists of QM, the menstrual art blog called Seeing Red Project, hosted on Wordpress. Seeing Red Project illustrates how QM participants found distinct paths in digital media to express certain politics that could not be fully explored from within the group's communicative platforms. The project was presented at the Queer Feminist Digital Media Praxis conference that I organised in 2013, and was described in the following terms: 'Seeing Red is a fairly regular photography project and blog exploring menstruation. It deals with social norms, sexuality and art, and hopes to unify as well as disgust. For the workshop, we will initiate a conversation about realness and authenticity online, using our own work as a starting point. How does menstrual activism translate into visual imagery, and how does it survive the squalor of the internet? For us, Seeing Red is about making visible the constant, but often hidden, experience of menstruation. It is recognising and reclaiming the visual strength and beauty in the accidental stain, the purposeful stain and the intimacy of blood' (Fotopoulou 2013b).

The project started in 2009 and involved presentation of own bleeding, always in connection with the body that bleeds. The artwork was exhibited mainly in academic settings and queer feminist anarcha/autonomous social spaces, but as the artists noted, the online version of the curated blog allowed many opportunities for receiving a range of feedback, from expressions of admiration to disgust and trolling. Receiving a steady flow of comments allowed them to explore the different meanings that their artistic work could have for audiences in context collapse. Anonymity allowed commentators to inhabit potentially any subject position, such as that of authority in defining art. But most importantly, for the creators the question of doing political art in an online medium was challenging.

Bibliography

Atton, C. (2002). *Alternative media*. London: SAGE.

Adamic, L., & State, B. (2015). The diffusion of support in an online social movement: Evidence from the adoption of equal-sign profile pictures. In

CSCW 15 proceedings of the 18th ACM conference on computer supported cooperative work & social computing (pp. 1741–1750). New York: ACM.

Anderson, B., & Fleckenstein, K. (2015). Virtual flag-bearing: Visual ideograph in digital media. http://www.brad-anderson.net/VirtualFlag-Bearing.pdf. Accessed 21 May 2016.

Appadurai, A. (1995). *Modernity at large: Cultural dimensions of globalization.* Minneapolis, MN: University of Minnesota Press.

Bell, L. (2013). Trigger warnings: Sex, lies and social justice utopia on Tumblr. *Networking Knowledge: Journal of the MeCCSA Postgraduate Network, 6*(1). http://ojs.meccsa.org.uk/index.php/netknow/article/view/296.

Bell, D., & Binnie, J. (2004). Authenticating queer space: Citizenship, urbanism and governance. *Urban Studies, 41,* 1807–1820.

Bell, D., & Valentine, G. (Eds.), (1995). *Mapping desire: Geographies of sexualities.* London: Routledge.

Berlant, L., & Freeman, E. (1992). Queer nationality. *Boundary 2, 19*(1), 149–180.

Berlant, L., & Warner, M. (1998). Sex in public. *Critical Inquiry, 24,* 547–566.

Binnie, J. (2010). Queer theory, neoliberalism and urban governance. In R. Leckey & K. Brooks (Eds.), *Queer theory: Law, culture, empire.* New York: Routledge.

Brighton & Hove Council. (2009). Housing strategy 2009–2014. Healthy homes, healthy lives, healthy city, LGBT (Lesbian Gay Bisexual and Trans) people's housing strategy executive summary: Brighton and Hove. http://www.brighton-hove.gov.uk/downloads/bhcc/LGBT_HS_2009-2014_-_Executive_Summary_%28draft%29.pdf. Accessed 10 August 2011.

Browne, K. (2006). Challenging queer geographies. *Antipode, 38*(5), 885–893.

Browne, K., & Lim, J. (2008). *Count me in too: LGBT lives in Brighton and Hove. Trans people: additional findings report.* Brighton: University of Brighton. http://www.brighton.ac.uk/cupp/images/stories/projects/cke/LGBTU/CMIT_Safety_Report_Final_Feb08.pdf.

Browne, K., Lim, J., & Brown, G. (2007). Introduction, or why have a book on geographies of sexualities?. In K. Browne, J. Lim, & G. Brown (Eds.), *Geographies of sexualities: Theory, practices and politics* (pp. 1–18). Farnham and Burlington: Ashgate.

BSSN. (2010) http://www.it.bton.ac.uk/bssn. Accessed 29 July 2011.

Campbell, B. (2004). Village people. *The Guardian.* 7 August. http://www.guardian.co.uk/world/2004/aug/07/gayrights.communities. Accessed 17 July 2011.

Casey, M. (2004). De-dyking queer space(s): Heterosexual female visibility in gay and lesbian spaces. *Sexualities, 7,* 446–461.

Christian. (2009). Session 1. Interviewed by Aristea Fotopoulou [MP3 audio recording] Brighton, 11th of February 2009. No transcript.

Costa, M. (2010). Pink pound's value rises in mainstream markets. *Marketing Week.* Centaur Media plc. 4 November. http://www.marketingweek.co.uk/

analysis/features/pink-pound%E2%80%99s-value-rises-in-mainstream-mar kets/3020077.article. Accessed 10 August 2011.

Count Me In. (2001). LGBT community strategy 2001–2006. http://www.spec trum-lgbt.org/downloads/count_me_in_strategy.pdf. Accessed 10 August 2011.

Crowley, M. S. (2010). How r u??? Lesbian and bi-identified youth on MySpace. *Journal of Lesbian Studies, 14*(1), 52–60.

Cvetkovich, A. (2003). *An archive of feeling: Trauma, sexuality and public cultures*. Durham, NC: Duke University Press.

Davies, H. (2005). The difference of queer. *Canadian Woman Studies/Les Cahiers De La Femme, 24*, 23–26.

De Ridder, S. (2015). Are digital media institutions shaping youth's intimacy stories? Strategies and tactics in the social networking site Netlog. *New Media & Society, 17*(3), 356–374.

Downes, J. et al. (Eds.), (2007). *Riot grrrl: Revolution girl style now!*. London: Black Dog.

Duggan, L. (2002). The new homonormativity: The sexual politics of neoliberalism. In R. Castronovo & D. D. Nelson (Eds.), *Materializing democracy: Toward a revitalized cultural politics*. Durham, NC: Duke University Press.

Duncan, N. (1996). Renegotiating gender and sexuality in public and private spaces. In N. Duncan (Ed.), *BodySpace: Destabilizing geographies of gender and sexuality* (pp. 127–145). New York: Routledge.

Engle, V. (pres.) (2006a). Lefties [videorecording] pt. 1, Property is theft. *BBC 4*, 2006.

Engle, V. (pres.) (2006b). Lefties [videorecording] pt. 2, Angry wimmin. *BBC 4*, 2006.

Fotopoulou, A. (2013a). Intersectionality' queer studies and hybridity: Methodological frameworks for social research. *Journal of International Women's Studies, 13*(2), 19–32. http://www.bridgew.edu/soas/jiws/Vol13_no2/.

Fotopoulou, A. (2013b). Seeing red project at the Queer fem media praxis workshop (17 May, Sussex). *Queer Social Media Praxis Conference Blog*. http:// queerfemdigiact.wordpress.com/2013/03/04/seeing-red-project-at-the-queer-fem-media-praxis-workshop-17-may-sussex/. Accessed 17 July 2016.

Francis (2009). No title. Interviewed by Aristea Fotopoulou [MP3 audio recording] Brighton, 6th March 2009.

Ghetto Brighton. (2009). http://www.ghettobrighton.com. Accessed 29 July 2009.

Giffney, N. (2004). Denormatizing queer theory. *Feminist Theory, 5*, 73–78.

Halberstam, J. (2005a). *In a queer time and place: Transgender bodies, subcultural lives*. New York: New York University Press.

Halberstam, J. (2005b). Shame and white gay masculinity. *Social Text, 23*, 219–233.

Hayles, N. K. (1999). *How we became posthuman virtual bodies in cybernetics, literature, and informatics*. Chicago, IL: University of Chicago Press.

Heckert, J., & Cleminson, R. (Eds.), (2011). *Anarchism & sexuality: Ethics, relationships and power*. New York: Routledge.

Henry, A. (2004). *Not my mother's sister: Generational conflict and third-wave feminism*. Bloomington: Indiana University Press.

Hodges, A. (2000). Gay liberation: 1970–2000. http://www.outgay.co.uk/glfintro.html. Accessed 17 July 2011.

Jackson, S., & Scott, S. (1996). *Feminism and sexuality: A reader*. Edinburgh: Edinburgh University Press.

Jenzen, O. (2016) Trans* and (gender) queer youth and online digital culture. Paper presented at the association of American Geographers annual meeting, 29 March–2 April 2016, San Francisco, USA.

Jenzen, O., & Karl, I. (2014). Make, share, care: Social media and LGBTQ youth engagement. *Ada: A Journal of Gender, New Media, and Technology 5*. http://adanewmedia.org/2014/07/issue5-jenzenkarl/.

Karatzogianni, A., & Kuntsman, A. (2012). *Digital cultures and the politics of emotion: Feelings, affect and technological change*. Basingstoke: Palgrave Macmillan.

Kates, S. M., & Belk, R. W. (2001). The meanings of lesbian and gay pride day. *Journal of Contemporary Ethnography, 30*, 392–429.

Kirsch, M. H. (2000). *Queer theory and social change*. London: Routledge.

Le Guin, U. (1974). *The dispossessed*. The Anarchist Library. http://theanarchistlibrary.org/library/ursula-k-le-guin-the-dispossessed.pdf. Accessed 17 July 2016.

Ledward, J. (2009) Editorial comment: Where is our pride? *Gscene*. 26 November. http://www.gscene.com/news/Editorial_Comment_Where_is_our_Pride.shtml. Accessed 10 August 2011.

Mac Bean, S. (2016). Being 'there': Contemporary London, Facebook and queer historical feeling. In S. Avery & K. M. Graham (Eds.), *Sex, time and place: Queer histories of London, c. 1850 to the present* (pp. 255–269). Bloomsbury: London.

Massey, D. B. (1994). *Space, place, and gender*. Minneapolis: University of Minnesota Press.

Matias, J. (2015). Were all those rainbow profile photos another Facebook study?. *The Atlantic*. http://www.theatlantic.com/technology/archive/2015/06/were-all-those-rainbow-profile-photos-another-facebook-experiment/397088/. Accessed 21 May 2016.

Mcinroy, L. B., & Craig, S. L. (2015). Transgender representation in offline and online media: LGBTQ youth perspectives. *Journal of Human Behaviour in the Social Environment, 22*, 606–617.

Mckay, G. (1996). *Senseless acts of beauty: Cultures of resistance since the sixties*. London: Verso.

Mckay, G. (1998). *DiY culture: Party & protest in nineties Britain*. London: Verso.

Morley, D. (2001). Belongings: Place, space and identity in a mediated world. *European Journal of Cultural Studies, 4*, 425–448.

Munt, S. (1998). *Heroic desire: Lesbian identity and cultural space*. New York: New York University Press.

Puar, J. K. (2002) Circuits of queer mobility: Tourism, travel, and globalization. *GLQ 8*, 101–137.

Pullen, C. (2014). *Queer youth and media cultures*. Basingstoke: Palgrave Macmillan.

Queen, C., & Schimel, L. (Eds.), (2001). *PoMoSEXUALS: Challenging assumptions about gender and sexuality*. San Francisco: Cleis Press.

Queer Mutiny Brighton (2006). Issue 1 [zine].

Queer Mutiny Brighton (2009). Queer Mutiny Manifesto [zine].

Queer Mutiny Brighton Wiki (2009). http://queermutinybrighton.wordpress.com/queer/. Accessed 17 July 2011.

Queeruption (2009). http://www.queeruption.org. Accessed 29 July 2011.

Raun, T. (2016). *Out online: Trans self-representation and community building on YouTube*. London: Routledge.

Reger, J. (ed.), (2005). *Different wavelengths: Studies of the contemporary women's movement*. London: Routledge.

Riseup Collective (2009). https://help.riseup.net/en. Accessed 17 July 2011.

Rubin, G. (1998). The miracle mile: South of market and gay male leather, 1962–1977. In J. Brook, C. Carlsson, & N. Peters (Eds.), *Reclaiming San Francisco: History, politics, culture*. San Francisco: City Lights Publishers.

Seidman, S. (1996). *Queer theory/sociology*. Cambridge, MA: Blackwell.

Shepard, B. (2002). *From ACT UP to the WTO: Urban protest and community building in the era of globalization*. London [u.a.]: Verso.

Sinfield, A. (1998). *Gay and after: Gender, culture and consumption*. London: Serpent's Tail.

Skeggs, B. (1999). *Matter Out of Place: Visibility and Sexualities in Leisure Spaces. Leisure Studies, 18*, 213–232

Smith, S. (1994). Mistaken identity—Or can identity politics liberate the oppressed? *International Socialism 62*. http://pubs.socialistreviewindex.org.uk/isj62/smith.htm. Accessed 25 April 2011.

Stephansen, H. C. (2016). Understanding citizen media as practice: Agents, processes, publics. In M. Baker & B. B. Blaagaard (Eds.), *Citizen media and public spaces* (pp. 25–41). London: Routledge.

Sundén, J. (2015). On trans-, glitch, and gender as machinery of failure. *First Monday, 20*, 4.

Tiidenberg, K., & Gomez Cruz, E. (2015). Selfies, image and the re-making of the body. *Body & Society*, *21*(4), 77–102.

Trans Media Watch (2010). How transgender people experience the media. http://www.transmediawatch.org/Documents/How%20Transgender% 20People%20Experience%20the%20Media.pdf. Accessed 20th July 2016.

Vivienne, S., & Burgess, J. (2013). The remediation of the personal photograph and the politics of self-representation in digital storytelling. *Journal of Material Culture*, *18*(3), 279–298.

Ward, J. (2003). Producing 'pride' in West Hollywood: A queer cultural capital for queers with cultural capital. *Sexualities*, *6*, 65–94.

Warner, M. (1993a). Introduction. In M. Warner (Ed.), *Fear of a queer planet: Queer politics and social theory*. Minneapolis: University of Minnesota Press.

CHAPTER 6

Epilogue: Looping Feminist Threads

Sustaining Knowledge, Creating Possibility

In this book, I set off to answer a key question – what do feminism and queer activism mean in the digital era, when digital technologies are so inextricably linked to culture, economy and politics?

By asking what feminism and queer activism are in the digital era, I have focused on the contradictions, tensions and often-paradoxical aspects of these politics, in relation to both identity and activist practice. I started from the premise that today both feminism, as forceful critique and praxis, and the figure of the feminist are often missing in digital as well as activism studies (with a few exceptions, see Jarrett 2016). When sexuality and gender politics do appear, or when *the feminist* is indeed invoked as a figure, it frequently seems like a finished project, a matter of the past that should be acknowledged ('I've been there, I know all about it'); or as niche intellectual interest, just for women and/or queer people; or as an omphaloscopic body of scholarly work and online media practice that speaks to those already committed to the identity of feminist, and who already have the cultural capital to participate in a specific type of middle-class, cis-gendered, white feminism.

What is lost in all these instances, I suggested, is feminism as an embodied activist practice that is performed through digitally connected networks and that articulates a political response to the new forms of governmentality that have appeared because of technoscientific accelera-tion. In this book, I argued that doing feminism and being feminist

© The Author(s) 2016   155
A. Fotopoulou, *Feminist Activism and Digital Networks*,
Palgrave Studies in Communication for Social Change,
DOI 10.1057/978-1-137-50471-5_6

involves enacting ourselves as activists – as embodied – and political subjects through media practices, technologies and their imaginaries. Thus my project of mapping contemporary feminist and queer formations was accompanied by important conceptual and analytical terms, which help us understand the complexities and contradictions of such politics in this context. First, with the notion of 'biodigital vulnerability', I aimed to make a case about the material/discursive conditions where feminist and queer political acts occur today at the convergence of digital and life (bio-) technologies. I argued that awareness of how problematic these conditions can be for women and/or queer people at a corporeal level, and public reflection in some way or another, can be empowering and productive. Such public articulation can bring people together, to mobilise and learn from one another, and therefore enables political subjectivity. Although the political struggles I mapped in this book tackle diverse issues and have different attachments and histories, the conditions of possibility that define them are both generative and prohibitive, and they are very similar. The focus of these politics on bodies, gender and sexuality across the themes of bodily autonomy, pornography, reproduction and queer social life connects them, as they attempt to formulate a critique of neoliberal conditions. Second, I used the umbrella term 'networked feminism' to describe this political project, with emphasis on the everyday negotiations with new communicative technologies. Through these negotiations, I argued, digital media technologies are problematised rather than accepted as intrinsically exploitative or empowering. My biopolitical approach and triple focus on practices, labour and imaginaries has thus allowed me to reach some significant findings about how activists make claims about rights online, and how they negotiate access, connectivity, openness and visibility in digital networks.

As we saw in Chapter 2, the London feminist groups and activists that I interviewed were not obsessed with updating their Facebook profiles, but they understood connectivity as the necessary pre-condition for having political voice in the dissonance of neoliberal politics. The adoption of new communication technologies and social networking within activist organisations seemed to be an indicator of 'keeping up', progress, newness and being present. It reflected a fear that older feminists and their histories were becoming excluded from political and social life. In this case, I argued that we need to challenge the assumed legitimacy of new communication technologies for activism, and that we should avoid using online presence as the measure of political engagement. As I have noted throughout the chapters of this book, although new media forms and network technologies permeate the individual and collective lives and practices of feminist and queer activists, slower ways of experiencing the world are still important to them. There is indeed a de-synchronisation between the political time of participatory practices of activists and the immediacy of digital media (Kaun 2015: 102). When the spokesperson of the SLFG humorously commented that meeting face-to-face was the organisation's Facebook, they essentially shattered the vision of unhindered and immediate citizen participation in Web 2.0. The priceless long discussions over meaning and priorities of action, the sometimes slow and tedious meetings, and at other times pleasurable community-building and educational parties of Queer Mutiny and anti-porn feminists, all took place at a different temporal regime to that of digital media and challenge the cultural assumptions that favour them. In fact, as the cases of this book exemplify, feminist and queer activists articulate their claims in a variety of media forms, varying from DIY zines, books and conferences and other cultural and political events, which reveal different temporalities of interaction, and engage different public worlds. These public worlds and asynchronous temporalities of interaction are entangled and are unevenly distributed across scales. Thus although digital media and social networking platforms in particular are today essential for protest, their characteristic immediacy is in fact detrimental for political identity because it simplifies how complex discourses are circulated (Barassi 2015: 85), whereas other non-digital media practices are more relevant in the everyday exchanges of women's and queer organisations.

It is imperative to challenge the assumption that feminist and queer activism has moved to the realm of the digital and is always connected for another reason. Not only do the widespread cultural understandings of participation and empowerment in relation to the digital technologies largely disregard the specificity of place and situated experience, it is also that such understandings are problematically fused with productivity, administrative control and functionality. The normalisation of doing *more,* of producing *more* with digital technologies and, as Judy Wajcman (2014) observes, in *Pressed for Time,* of being increasingly busy, harried and short for time,[1] is indeed an ideological tool in contemporary digital capitalism. Today, not only activists but also professionals, students and unemployed people are expected to be digitally connected, regardless of age or level of media literacy; they are expected to be prepared to perform financial transactions, to communicate and advocate over the internet.[2]

Put simply, exclusions after Web 2.0 and in the era of the Internet of Things, is not plainly a case of access and being online or offline, as was the case in the beginning of the 2000s. Exclusions are more sophisticated and concern productivity, immediacy and visibility – the frequency of updating online presence, producing and sharing more interesting content in social media. The question thus remains: do we aspire to a form of feminist and queer activism that is communicated immediately, and measured by how productive we are, how often our organisation's page is being updated and how many 'likes' and shares it has received?

There is indeed a danger to foreground often prescribed and consensual forms of political engagement, because in digital networked media the complexity of social arrangements and situated experience are simplified, while the self-defining capacities of activist groups are narrowed down. But it is not just the complexity of political identity and the density of everyday social relationships in activist spaces that the logic of the network more generally, and the affordances of digital media platforms in particular, cannot fully accommodate. As the examples in Chapters 3 and 4 presented in relation to feminist politics around pornography and reproductive rights respectively, feminism has historically grounded its critical projects in situated experience. The experiences of living as a body with passions and feelings, and the focus on life and modes of living have historically shaped feminist and queer political projects at a fundamental level. Motivated by the need and desire to start from subjective experience, in consciousness raising meetings for instance, feminism has produced bodies of knowledge that have challenged dominant truths about technoscience (see Murphy 2012). Although some of these practices have lost their traction and relevance to todays' organising as technoscience has also moved on, the focus on sharing experiences of subordination, and on subjective experience as starting points for the production of knowledge remains. In this book, hashtag feminism, postporn cultures and events, queer pedagogies and websites where repro-technologies are debated are some examples of contemporary forms of feminism and queer activism whose key project revolves around the production of knowledge. The practices of producing this knowledge meant that feminist and queer activists, on the one hand, critiqued the logic of digital networking technologies, and its centrality in digital capitalism, and on the other, used them in order to circulate their counter-narratives and versions of the world, while labouring. A key contribution that this book hopes to make is to account for how this contradiction is central in the project of contemporary feminism and queer politics.

The book shows how feminist and queer politics materialise as biopolitical projects at the complex intersections of bodies and technologies, sometimes in networks and sometimes off the network, in particular localities. In each case, these formations created their own meanings about what constitutes legitimate political communication and developed their own organisational practices, with and without digital media technologies. Some voluntarily resisted belonging to a network, some were excluded for various reasons, some decided to discontinue their connections and some did all of the above, but in different networks. These *paranodals*, as Mejias (2013) calls those who do not conform to the logic of the network and disturb the digital world, challenge nodocentrism. They also remind us that nonparticipation (or modular participation) is a mode of resistance to the very idea of digital networks and the ways they operationalise the everyday realities of doing activism. Therefore, another implicit claim of the book is that technologies are not autonomous technological systems but digital networks that are constituted through phenomenological and embodied, cultural and social entanglements. Digital technologies in this understanding are produced within, and themselves produce meaning-making practices.

Mapping existing feminist and queer formations, and telling a story about them has led me to rethink knowledge-making and responsibility, as a feminist project in itself. I have navigated in very different contexts, spaces, and scales with web crawling, discourse analysis, in-depth interviewing, participant observation and digital ethnographic methods. This way the book responded to a clear need in the literature for systematic, ethnographic analyses of feminist and queer media and communication. Through this empirical exploration and through this text, I did not catalogue what was already there; I foregrounded certain questions and issues over others while trying to allow political futures to unravel. My attention on materiality privileged humans (women and queer bodies) and their social worlds, not digital networks; in the context of accelerated biodigital capitalism, women are the sources both of biological raw material, for example, eggs, and biovalue through their labour, for example, in online porn. But instead of foregrounding the particularities of individual organisations or activist groups, I have traced a topographic path that marks the relative positions of these groups and their dynamic relationships at a particular moment in time. Sometimes these relationships were antagonistic; sometimes they were projects of alliance building and solidarity; and often they were overlapping and across time. Methodologically then, a significant contribution of this book is its effort to account for the contradictions that characterise the multiple forms of feminist activism emerging in the context of digital capitalism. A tacit topographic approach has allowed me to problematise notions of representativeness, identity and difference, as these are expressed across political fields, and to additionally make wider claims about what communicative practices and digital media technologies mean for feminist and queer politics.

Meanwhile, by pulling threads from different theoretical positions and epistemological fields, I have followed Donna Haraway's (1997: 268–271) invitation to convey my research as if I participate in a collective project of producing responsible and accountable feminist knowledge, guided by the metaphor of the cat's cradle game. This game of looping threads between disciplinary fields of political science, cultural studies, media theory, and science and technology studies is an inherent part of the theoretical exploration of this book. These approaches, when brought together, often create tensions – not least because of their own different intellectual attachments. I am aware of these tensions, but still think that research needs to be conducted with a playful attitude and to transcend disciplinary rules in order to enable new routes of understanding of the performative production of political subjectivities and realities.

Since I started research for this book, there has been a notable proliferation of online sites and social networking platforms by feminist and queer groups. Austerity measures affecting feminist and queer academics and activists in the UK,[3] but also, changes in biotechnologies and their regulation, signal how doing queer politics and being feminist is bound to transform in more fundamental ways than we imagined ten years ago. But the themes that this book raised, namely the complex intersection of mediation and politicisation, embodiment and information, technology and culture, are on-going concerns. Communicative and biotechnological capitalism continues to define the material conditions for making meaning about what politics and activism is, and for negotiating understandings of gender, sexuality, human and nonhuman. Thus, although this book and the empirical cases it accounts for are clearly situated within a historical and sociopolitical context, the problematic it raises are relevant and on-going.

It is important to keep asking questions about what we aspire and imagine for the future of feminism and queer activism in a fast-changing and ever so dense communicative environment of connections. Today, the material practices of making feminist and queer memory are changing, as personal narratives, oral histories and ephemera are increasingly being digitally archived and exhibited online and in spaces such as the British Library.[4]

As a result, the past is ever more present. An implicit claim of this book was that thinking about these overlapping configurations of time, and how different asynchronous temporalities (of different histories, of organising for protest, of communicating, of socialising) can help us challenge binaries of 'new' and 'old'; they can also restore the medium in the process of mediation, and to importantly reinstate the media as constant material agents in the process of politicisation. While digital networks help us maintain a dialogue with the past, feminism creates conditions of possibility in the present, for a livable future – by making claims for rights, and social justice, across networks, media and technologies. These are the recursive loops of feminism across time, that link past, present and future. At a time of 'post'-prefixes, when feminism, identity and even the digital are considered completed processes or empty signifiers,[5] it is important to be reminded about the multi-layered networks and relationships that sustain feminist knowledge and identity. In a world of increasing interconnectedness, where things and people create data for public authorities and for corporations, today more than ever feminism is not only necessary but vital.

NOTES

1. Wajcman (2014) notes how acceleration of technological innovation in digital capitalism has made us feel that we are short of time. Multitasking, she argues, with our digital devices and appearing as if we are always busy has become a form of status amongst middle-class professionals and has made leisure time disappear.
2. We have analysed expectations of expertise in Bassett et al. (2015).
3. What I have in mind here is educational cuts affecting particularly the humanities disciplines and gender studies in universities around the UK, but also the funding cuts affecting charitable organisations, like Rape Crisis Centres.
4. See, for example the project *Sisterhood and After: An Oral History of the UK Women's Liberation Movement,* the first national oral history archive of the post-1968 women's movement, funded by the Leverhulme Trust 2010–2013.
5. I refer here to post-feminism, and to the 'postdigital' turn, see Bassett (2015).

BIBLIOGRAPHY

Barassi, V. (2015). Social media, immediacy and the time for democracy: Critical reflections on social media as 'temporalizing practices'. In L. Dencik & O. Leistert (Eds.), *Critical perspectives on social media and protest: Between control and emancipation.* London: Rowman & Littlefield.

Bassett, C. (2015). Not now? Feminism, technology, postdigital. In *Postdigital aesthetics* (pp. 136–150). UK: Palgrave Macmillan.

Bassett, C., Fotopoulou, A., & Howland, K. (2015). Expertise: A report and a manifesto. *Convergence, 21*(3), 328–342. http://www.scopus.com/inward/record.url?eid=2-s2.0-84938271985&partnerID=40&md5=81fb98620628957e3e05314b3aece240.

Haraway, D. J. (1997). *ModestWitness@secondMillennium. FemaleManMeets OncoMouse: Feminism and technoscience.* New York: Routledge.

Jarrett, K. (2016). *Feminism, labour and digital media: The digital housewife.* London: Routledge.

Kaun, A. (2015). 'This space belongs to us!': Protest spaces in times of accelerating capitalism. In L. Dencik & O. Leistert (Eds.), *Critical perspectives on social media and protest: Between control and emancipation.* London: Rowman & Littlefield.

Mejias, U. (2013). *Off the network.* Minneapolis: University of Minnesota Press.

Murphy, M. (2012). *Seizing the means of reproduction: Entanglements of feminism, health, and technoscience.* Duke University Press.

Wajcman, J. (2014). *Pressed for time: The acceleration of life in digital capitalism.* University of Chicago Press.

INDEX

© The Author(s) 2016
A. Fotopoulou, *Feminist Activism and Digital Networks*,
Palgrave Studies in Communication for Social Change,
DOI 10.1057/978-1-137-50471-5

163

Printed by Printforce, the Netherlands